ONE STEP AHEAD

The FJMC Influence on the Conservative/Masorti Movement

A *Festschrift* written in honor of
Rabbi Charles Simon

Edited by Daniel M. Kimmel

fjmc THE FEDERATION OF JEWISH MEN'S CLUBS, INC.

In Gratitude

This Festschrift would not have been possible without the generous support of the individuals and organizations listed below.

DOUBLE DIAMOND LEVEL - $25,000
FJMC Foundation for Jewish Life

DIAMOND LEVEL - $15,000
Brand Foundation (Bart Kogan)

PLATINUM LEVEL - $10,000
Anonymous

GOLD LEVEL - $5000 - 9999
Dr. Gary & Leah Smith and Richard & Lillian Gray - Best Friends of FJMC
Claudio & Penny Pincus
New York Metro Region of FJMC
Western Region of FJMC
New England Region of FJMC
Hudson Valley Region of FJMC

SILVER LEVEL - $2500 - 4999
Northern New Jersey Region of FJMC
Lake Ontario Region of FJMC
Keruv Family - (see page 5)

TRIBUTE LEVEL - $1000 - 2499
Allen Hyman, Hyman Family Charitable Foundation
JB & Lynette Mazer
Eric & Fern Weis
Jeffrey Goldberg
Greg & Linda Gore
Norman* & Joan Kurtz
Bob Braitman* & Bonnie Gordon
Ruthy & Gene Sacks
Rabbi Jaymee Alpert
Dr. Jerome* and Estelle Agrest
Myles* & Gail Simpson
Allan* & Caren Gottesman
Mike* & Shirley Mills
Tom Sudow and family
Midwest Region of FJMC
Kentucky-Indiana-Ohio Region of FJMC
Steve Neustein and Warren Sufrin
The International Kiddush Club
Roy & Geri Liemer
Rabbi Simon's Minyan Group - (see page 6)

* Past International President of the FJMC

Rabbi's Tribute

"Select a rabbi for yourself, and acquire a friend" (Ethics of the Fathers 1:6). Thank you, Chuck, for being both a rabbi and a friend to so, so many of us.

Elliot Dorff

ABRAHAM LEVEL
Rabbi Jaymee Alpert

SOLOMON LEVEL
Rabbi Stewart Vogel

KING DAVID LEVEL
Rabbi Irvin Wise
Rabbi Nathanial Esray
Rabbi Jeffrey Abraham
Rabbi Daniel Stein
Rabbi Eytan Hammerman
Rabbi Mitch Levine and Agudis Achim Brotherhood
Rabbi Aaron Schonbrun
Rabbi Ari Isenberg-Grzeda
Rabbi Steven E. Kane
Rabbi David Wolpe
Rabbi Daniel Lieben
Rabbi Elliot Dorff
Rabbi Stuart Weinblatt
Rabbis David Lerner & Michael Fel

MAIMONIDES LEVEL
Rabbi Elana Zelony
Rabbi Neil Cooper
Rabbi Neil Sandler
Rabbi Eric Yanoff
Rabbi Eric Solomon
Rabbi Murray Ezring
Rabbi Leonard Gordon

CANTOR'S TRIBUTE
Cantor's Assembly
Cantor Alberto Mizrahi

Keruv Family

SILVER LEVEL - $2500

David Kaplan
Dave Mogul
Dr. Gary & Leah Smith
Richard & Lillian Gray
Gene Sacks
Phil & Sheryl Snyder
Joshua & Kari Kohn
Liz Cox
Alayne Pick
Elise Leonard & Arnold Semel
Lynn Wolfe
Stephen Lachter
Stuart & Nancy Schlossman
Jeffrey & Anita Landau
Sharon Felix
Arthur & Shelley Spar
Arthur & Eileen Lashin
Alan Budman
Michael Frelich
Elaine Krutchik
Harvey & Barbara Braunstein
Greg Gore
Linda Romano
Alex Romano

Rabbi Simon's Minyan Group

RABBI SIMON'S MINYAN GROUP - TRIBUTE LEVEL - $1000 - 2499

Mitchel & Laurie Liner
Ronald & Narion Stein
James & Elisabeth Baron
Alfred & Joann Ivry
Michael and Ramella & Sharon Strassfeld
Helena Diamont Glass
Jacob & Marine Halpern
Harvey & Cynthia May
James & Patricia Fingeroth
Marvin & Helene Peretz
Jim & Liz Baron
Dan Stern*
Benjamin and Barbara Zucker

* Past International President of the FJMC

TABLE OF CONTENTS

PREFACE: What is a *Festschrift?* – Daniel M. Kimmel 9

INTRODUCTION: Growing Up With The Men's Clubs – 11
Dr. Rela Mintz Geffen

THE CONSERVATIVE/MASORTI MOVEMENT: 14
Who Is Really In Charge? – Rabbi Charles Simon

THE VOLUNTEER CULTURE 18

WHY RISK RAISING YOUR HAND? Putting Volunteerism In 19
Perspective – Excerpt from Building a Successful Volunteer Culture

JEWISH LEADERSHIP: Bibilical & Modern – 22
Rabbi Dr. Bradley Shavit Artson

CREATING A RUACH CULTURE – Dr. Burton L. Fischman 31

THE OFFICAL® HISTORY OF THE INTERNATIONAL 33
KIDDUSH CLUB – Stan Greenspan

THE SECRET SAUCE: Fostering A Grassroots Structure – 37
Rabbi Charles Simon

THE INITIATIVES: 39
HOW THE FJMC HAS MADE A DIFFERENCE

IT STARTS WITH HEBREW LITERACY – Daniel M. Kimmel ... 40

THE ART OF JEWISH LIVING – Dr. Ron Wolfson 45

THE YELLOW CANDLE™: The Idea That Shaped Holocaust ... 49
Programming – Eric Weis

THE WORLD WIDE WRAP – Michael Abadi 57

KERUV: OPENING THE DOORS OF THE SYNAGOGUE – ... 62
Harvey Braunstein

TABLE OF CONTENTS (CON'T)

BUILDING SHABBAT COMMUNITY – Norm Kurtz ... 74

THE WELLNESS CHALLENGE – Dr. Robert E. Braitman ... 79

A MATCH MADE IN HEAVEN: THE RAMAH/FJMC
PARTNERSHIP – Richard Skolnik ... 83

HEARING MEN'S VOICES: A CASE STUDY ... 88

IN THE BEGINNING – Rabbi Seymour Rosenbloom ... 89

GOING STRONG AFTER TWENTY YEARS –
Dr. Robert E. Braitman ... 93

MAKING IT YOUR OWN – Dr. Paul Davidson ... 96

APPENDIX : I LOVE CHUCK ... 102

PREFACE

WHAT IS A *FESTSCHRIFT?*

If you're not in the rarefied world of academia you have probably never heard of a *Festschrift.* Developed in Germany in the early 20th century, it was brought over to the United States by scholarly refugees and became a custom here without losing its original name. Essentially it is a volume like this one, a collection of essays honoring a scholar upon reaching a milestone such as – in the case of Rabbi Charles Simon – his retirement after 35 years as executive director of the Federation of Jewish Men's Clubs. What it is not is a "tribute book," where friends wish him luck, send him love, and otherwise focus on the person being honored. Thus if you submitted something along those lines you will have to look in the appendix at the back of this volume, where we preserved some of the outpouring of love and friendship for him.

What Rabbi Simon asked for, and what I have put together with the help of the generous written and financial contributions that came in for this volume, is a celebration of the numerous initiatives that the FJMC has undertaken during his tenure. When one considers the relative size of our organization compared to the branches of Conservative Judaism, it's quite amazing how often the FJMC has initiated or changed the conversation in our movement. In the coming pages you will encounter the histories of these various initiatives as well as comments and quotes "from the record" that illustrate, in various ways, the impact they have had.

The motto of the FJMC is that it is about "involving Jewish men in Jewish life." Under Rabbi Simon's leadership ideas have percolated up from individual clubs, been shaped and adapted by the organization, and then offered widely to member clubs who have made them their own, often coming up with additional ways to expand or strengthen the program.

In each instance, a lack was perceived or a challenge was unmet, and the FJMC under Rabbi Simon didn't ask why someone didn't do something, but instead showed what could be done. Were our members unengaged by Jewish services and rituals? A Hebrew literacy campaign showed how Jewish men in our clubs could be recruited to teach others basic Hebrew literacy so they could follow and participate in our services. A series of books – **The Art of Jewish Living** – modeled the Passover seder and Shabbat home rituals which our members could incorporate into their family's lives. The annual

World Wide Wrap put the mitzvah of tefillin back into the mainstream of Conservative practice. The Yellow Candle initiative established Holocaust remembrance and education as part of the agenda for not only Conservative congregations, but for other branches of the Jewish community and even for non-Jews.

The FJMC has not limited itself to religious observances, recognizing that it serves its members by touching all parts of their lives. Initiatives on men's health issues grew out of "Hearing Men's Voices," where it was recognized that men needed a place to open up on issues they rarely shared with others: being a father and being a son, dealing with the stresses of work, and in what was initially one of the most controversial measures, launching discussions on Keruv, reaching out and welcoming non-Jewish family members with the goal of creating and strengthening Jewish families. More recently, the FJMC has launched an initiative focusing on family finances, both as a means of education on subjects like "living wills" but also as a way of transmitting Jewish values when it comes to financial matters such as saving, charitable donations, and preparing for the future.

Rabbi Simon – or Chuck, as many of the people reading this call him in love and friendship – may not appear on every page of this *Festschrift*, although he has contributed some material himself and is mentioned in the context of his involvement with the various FJMC initiatives during his tenure. However don't be fooled. This entire book, put together in his honor, could be considered the biography of his professional life. These are the ideas that were brought up during his stewardship and through his efforts – and, as he'd be the first to admit – the efforts of countless people at the international as well as the local level, transformed the FJMC into what it is today: a powerful leader for innovation and renewal in the Conservative movement.

In following his lead, it is my hope as editor of this volume that readers will be inspired not only by the FJMC's past successes over the last 35 years, but will take from this the notion that when it comes to providing leadership for the Jewish community in the 21st century, our story is still unfolding.

Daniel M. Kimmel is an author and journalist in Somerville, Massachusetts who served as master of ceremonies for the New England Region of the FJMC and as editor of the Jewish Advocate. He edited the **Work and Worth** volume of the "Hearing Men's Voices" series.

INTRODUCTION
GROWING UP WITH THE MEN'S CLUBS

It is a particular pleasure to write this introduction as I was probably the only preteen girl in America to know about the Federation of Jewish Mens Clubs, to read "The Torch" magazine, and to attend many of the FJMC conventions. This came about because, among the several responsibilities of my beloved father, Rabbi Joel S. Geffen, was a directive from Rabbi Louis Finkelstein, his boss (as my intrepid mother referred to him) at the Jewish Theological Seminary of America (JTSA). Rabbi Finkelstein asked him to create and nurture the Federation of Jewish Men's Clubs. He wanted to make sure that, as Conservative congregations were founded around the country, both individual local men and their groups would develop relationships as a national organization, thus linking their members more strongly to the Conservative movement.

Our family, including my mother, my older sister Lisa, and myself (not yet two) moved to New York City in 1945 when, after eighteen years and having founded two congregations, my father left his pulpit in Troy, New York. He was recruited by JTSA to work with Rabbi Max Arzt as assistant director of field activities and community education. Together, he and Rabbi Arzt founded many Conservative congregations and becoming the core of the development department. Later, for ten years, he added the title of director of the Metropolitan Region of the United Synagogue and, finally, director of the men's clubs. Outside of New York City this last title was the one for which he was best known. His last important strategic act was to ensure a future for the FJMC by recruiting Rabbi Charles Simon to be his partner and future director of the FJMC.

It is always important to study trends within the American Jewish community against the backdrop of American society more generally. American Jews are surely as American as they are Jewish. Within the broad anti-sexism, pro gender-equality ideology so prevalent in the country at large, the Federation of Jewish Men's Clubs appeared, by the late 1980s, to be waging countercultural struggles in a number of arenas. The two most controversial were first, a more positive view than the rest of the Conservative/Masorti movement of the potential role of interfaith families in the synagogue and Jewish cultural life and, second, the positive role of all-male groups (i.e., "Men's Clubs/Brotherhoods"). Its leadership, both lay and professional, advocated for the efficacy of men's groups and the positive aspects of separation by gender.

Reconceptualization of gender roles in American society has preoccupied scholars and laypeople alike at the end of the twentieth and beginning of the twenty-first centuries. The expansion, contraction and exchange of roles of women and men has been the focus of intellectual analysis as well as the examination of day-to-day behavior. There has been heavy emphasis on changes in the identity and lives of women, whether single or married, in the home or in the workplace, in the polity or in educational institutions. The impact of these changes on religious institutional life as well as home ritual participation has been pervasive.

Within the International FJMC several nationwide projects took hold. These projects – along with the annual and later biennial conventions, and the organization of a strong, committed national board, many of whom became devotees of my father – fulfilled the original vision of Rabbi Finkelstein of binding these men to the Conservative movement and developing an "on ramp" to leadership of the United Synagogue.

Men around the country encouraged activities such as the laying on of tefillin by youth and adults, Shoah commemorations through a special candle program, and support of Camps Ramah through organization of annual concerts for Ramah in the Poconos and luncheons honoring teen leaders in Los Angeles and the San Fernando Valley. It is important to note that the World Wide Wrap tefillin program was open to women and men just as prayer leadership at FJMC conventions were among the earliest to include egalitarian services. Later, under Rabbi Simon, the Federation developed a special relationship with the Cantors Institute and added Jewish music to its focus. Although the Cantors Institute and Cantors Assembly were undergoing their own struggles over gender roles, various leading cantors participated at the national conventions of the FJMC.

Laymen and professionals were trained to work with interfaith families in their own synagogues – a countercultural effort that led to criticism of Rabbi Simon and of the organization as a whole. Although the criticism persisted, Rabbi Simon and "his" men persevered. Only in the last decade has the critique softened. Regular institutes were held with regional and national groups of rabbis and laypeople training them to handle the psychological ramifications of parenting and grandparenting in interfaith households, and how to do effective synagogue, home holiday and social celebrations. All of these efforts were aimed at mainstreaming converts and their partners into synagogue life.

Though the controversy over highlighting a men's group was more subtle and though there was no negative reaction over the persistence of sisterhoods, there is no doubt that the focus on men's clubs was cause for critique. Some attempts at joint programming were made, including a combined movement magazine, however the efforts were limited and short-lived. There were jointly sponsored synagogue activities such as classes, lecture series and sports nights, but calendars, special sabbaths, and even some book groups often remained limited to one gender or another. No attempts were made at joint conventions, trips to Israel or Elderhostel type programs.

Rabbi Simon has continued and advanced the work of the FJMC. He has not shied away from controversy while continuing the vision first embraced by Rabbi Louis Finkelstein and my father. Let us all hope that it will be further enhanced in the future by the generations to come of Jews devoted to the Conservative/Masorti movement.

Dr. Rela Mintz Geffen, Philadelphia, Pennsylvania
Dr. Geffen is the daughter of Rabbi Joel S. Geffen, who served as an advisor to the FJMC for 40 years.

THE CONSERVATIVE/MASORTI MOVEMENT:
WHO IS REALLY IN CHARGE?

To an outsider the Conservative/Masorti movement may appear to be monolithic, but as this brief history shows, it's more like a family: all on the same side but sometimes working at cross-purposes. It doesn't have to be that way. Here Rabbi Charles Simon reflect back on the modern history of the movement as seen from the perspective of the Federation of Jewish Men's Clubs.

Let me begin by stating that it is my firm belief that professional leaders of Conservative movement organizations are serious, dedicated, and hardworking individuals. Unfortunately they have been shaped by the cultures of their respective organizations in a manner that hinders the development of the Conservative movement, limiting us to a number of independent organizations loosely guided by the Committee of Jewish Law and Standards of the Rabbinical Assembly. In an ideal world each of the arms of the movement would be able to come up with innovative ideas that would strengthen Conservative Judaism as a whole, but that is not the case. Whether by happenstance or design, that is not what has occurred. Let me set forth how I believe this has happened.

In the days of Chancellors Louis Finkelstein and Gerson Cohen, the Jewish Theological Seminary of America was referred to as "The Fountainhead of Conservative Judaism." Scholars, rabbis, cantors, and teachers were educated there and from there they went on to pulpits, university classrooms, and a variety of Jewish schools and organizations. They were giants who helped define what it meant to be an American Jew. It was Dr. Finkelstein who gifted President Harry S Truman with a Torah, a symbolic gesture but one which signified the recognition of the Jews as part of the American community. The Conservative Movement was growing. Arthur Bruckman, president of the FJMC (then called the National Federation of Jewish Men's Clubs), joined by a representative of the Women's League, Bessie Aaronson, and her husband, Rabbi David Aaronson, were instrumental in expanding the movement to western Pennsylvania, Texas and California in 1949. It was a time of growth.

It was during this period that the "joint campaign" was created. It would continue until 2016. It began during 1943-1944 and consisted of a partnership between the Seminary, United Synagogue (then called the United Synagogue of America) and the Rabbinical Assembly. As it was structured, the joint campaign favored the Seminary, placing United Synagogue in a minor position. Dr. Finkelstein strengthened the Seminary's role when, in 1943, he engaged Rabbi Joel Geffen to travel to communities across the country and help build men's clubs at member congregations. Rabbi Geffen's actions revitalized the NFJMC, which had been created in 1929, and developed a cadre that was loyal to the Seminary. The Berman board room and the Rosenshine auditorium at JTS were named after vice presidents of the NFJMC. I suspect that it was the tension that developed from the desire for funds that was one of the primary causes for the development of and hardening of the different cultures of each organization in the partnership. Once formed, these attitudes were nearly impossible to be reconstructed.

Former Vice Chancellor and Finkelstein scholar Rabbi Michael Greenbaum summed it up thusly:

> In 1943-44... the joint campaign emerged out of a year long debate within and among the [United Synagogue, the Rabbinic Assembly, and the Seminary] for interorganizational agreement. The creation of the Liaison Committee also came from these discussions. The joint campaign was called "Campaign for the Jewish Theological Seminary in cooperation with the United Synagogue and Rabbinical Assembly."

The NFJMC was re-created by JTS to develop lay leaders who would also be Seminary supporters, thus ensuring that the congregational arm wouldn't overshadow the training institution. I believe that the structure of the joint campaign and the subsequent creation of the Women's League and FJMC (both of which broke away from United Synagogue in the 1950's and early 1960's) were core reasons for the lack of a unified Conservative movement.

With the appointment of Dr. Gerson Cohen as chancellor in the early 1980's, the tension between the Seminary, the RA and the USCJ increased. The question of who spoke for the movement became a constant question which would never be resolved. While cooperation in some areas was necessary and happened as a matter of course (e.g., placement of rabbis and cantors, representation on the Law committee), requests to alter the balance of the joint campaign was just one of many issues between the organizations that fostered competition rather than cooperation. The competition between the USCJ, RA, and JTS were mirrored by the relationship between the USCJ, WLCJ and FJMC. As the FJMC began to innovate and deliver various programmatic initiatives, (the Hebrew Literacy Campaign, the Art of Jewish Living series and the Yom HaShoah Yellow Yarhtzeit candle observance), the relationship between the USCJ and FJMC became more tenuous. Ironically, as a result of who ascended to leaderership of both the FJMC and WLCJ, the partnership between the movement's men's clubs and sisterhoods increased and developed into one of warmth and mutual respect.

By the 1980's the cultures of the arms of the movement had been firmly established and solidified. The professional leadership which replaced (in the first decade of the 21st century) Dr. Cohen, Rabbi Epstein, and Rabbi Meyers could only have been altered if each party agreed to limit its autonomy. With attitudes and procedure locked in after decades of practice, the act of rethinking and redeveloping the intraorganizational relationships was something which all parties refused to do.

The movement's leaders were not blind to the problem. There was an attempt to bridge the gap between the various Conservative organizations which was the creation of the LCCJ, the Leadership Council of Conservative Judaism. Rabbi Michael Greenbaum and I were the catalysts for the creation this body. The LCCJ served as the only body that brought the leadership of every organization in the movement together several times a year. The LCCJ was not without its successes. It developed a movement calendar, a list of publications, a statement on intermarriage, a coordinated response on various matters at the GA (general assembly of Jewish organizations) as well as a number of other items. It established a cost for membership and for a number of years supported a number of committees.

At one point the USCJ withdrew because it objected to all LCCJ meetings taking place at the Seminary and chaired by the Chancellor. A compromise was reached after two years and USCJ agreed to return if the Chair rotated amongst the five founding bodies, JTS, RA, USCJ, FJMC and WLCJ. The LCCJ functioned for nearly twenty years until the change of leadership in the RA, JTS and USCJ resulted in a new group of leaders, each with the burden of a new organization upon their shoulders coupled with a lack of understanding of the nature and culture of the involved parties. Sadly the result was the dissolution of the LCCJ in 2015.

After 36 years working on behalf of the movement and after promoting the unity of the movement, I have come to view the movement in a different light, one that I think is important to share. Rabbi Mordecai Waxman, (author of Tradition and Change and founder of the World Council of Synagogues, now called Masorti Olami), has described us as a series of organizations united only in the values we sought to perpetuate based on our own understandings of how we perceived Jewish life. I agree. This vision of a movement has the potential to empower every organization to do more, to seek new ways to address existing and emerging needs. The only thing which limits us is our vision. Rather than seeing ourselves in competititon for control of the movement as a whole, we need to see ourselves in parallel lanes, all heading to the same goal. When we help or inspire each other, it is not a loss for our "track," it is a victory for the movement as a whole. The FJMC cannot presume to speak for the entire Conservative movement. However for the last several decades it has engaged in one initiative after another that has strengthened our movement far beyond our men's clubs. As we look to the future, it is a role that I hope the FJMC will continue to play.

Rabbi Charles Simon served as the executive director of the FJMC from 1983 to 2017.

THE VOLUNTEER CULTURE

Outside of its small office in New York, the FJMC relies entirely on volunteers, who tackle everything from international, regional, and local leadership roles, to taking on the various tasks requires for a club program, a regional event, or the biennial convention. This section explores the special issues that such activities raise from recruiting volunteers to inspiring them to continued involvement.

WHY RISK RAISING YOUR HAND?
PUTTING VOLUNTEERISM IN PERSPECTIVE

Volunteering isn't always easy.

How many times have people risked raising their hand only to have it figuratively slapped so hard it stung? I'd say almost as often as chicken is served at a Friday night Shabbat dinner. And how often has someone who is highly motivated indicated a willingness to volunteer only to be ignored? Perhaps not as often as chicken appears on the Shabbat table, but still far too often.

Volunteering definitely has its challenges. So does dealing with volunteers. Moreover, the challenges are completely different from those faced in conventional employer-employee relationships.

Volunteers are valuable commodities to any organization, but they need to be handled with care. They have limited time and are not necessarily interested in assuming leadership roles, regardless of how well they perform. People volunteer for different reasons, and executive-level not-for-profit professionals require specific talents and broad vision to weave together the different personalities and skill sets before them into a coherent, functioning volunteer culture.

In most cases, volunteers can't be fired. They are not business-world interns who can be dismissed at will. They are usually members of the community who have willingly come forward. Dismissing them inappropriately or alienating them can damage an organization's reputation in the community.

Volunteerism builds relationships and communities. In my eyes, it is a core Jewish value that dates to Mishnaic (Greco-Roman) times. Volunteering broadens our worldview and helps make us better people. Key to this process is cultivating motivated volunteers and teaching those who run not-for-profits how to build healthy, vibrant volunteer cultures. Two incidents in my early career challenged and shaped my thinking.

The first was a 1974 seminar organized for rabbinical students at The Jewish Theological Seminary in New York, where I was studying at the time. It featured Leonard Greenberg, a former co-owner of Coleco Toys, as the principal speaker. Leonard's topic was "Marketing Jewish Life." The focus of his presentation was that we, as future rabbis, needed to understand the leisure-time market because we were in direct competition with it for the attention of our congregants. He explained that to attract people to our synagogues, we needed to develop a marketing strategy and view our successes as direct results of our sales efforts.

Leonard spoke a language that few of us understood. Yet it struck a chord. I realized that if I were to be successful in my rabbinate, my thinking needed to shift from believing that a rabbi was a person who taught mitzvot to understanding that a rabbi was a person who marketed Jewish living.

The second incident occurred around 1982 while I was serving my second congregation. I was the associate rabbi for a congregation in upstate New York. After I had served for a year, my senior colleague decided to take a long-deserved sabbatical and travel for six months.

A few weeks later, I began instituting minor changes. As an associate I couldn't tamper with major policies. But there were a number of smaller issues I felt I could and should address. Consider the following: at most synagogues the Shabbat service unfolds on a stage we call the bima. The services are well choreographed, include dramatic and less dramatic moments, and are usually conducted by two principal actors, the rabbi and the cantor. Supporting roles are filled by people who recite special prayers, and readings, or are part of the choreography of the Torah service.

I began by modifying the choreography and eventually began to tweak the script. One week, I changed a tune. The following week, I led a discussion instead of delivering a sermon. Once, the cantor and I successfully challenged the congregation to become active participants. My small acts of rebellion – which seem so commonplace today but were nearly revolutionary back in the early 1980s – created a ripple effect. The synagogue was now growing and infused with new passion. To meet the demands of an increased student body, I found myself recruiting new teachers, quite a challenge in a community two hours north of New York City.

I made lists of people who were minimally active in the synagogue but were engaged in what I considered interesting pursuits. They were academics, musicians, artists, lawyers, and shopkeepers. I called each of them arranged to visit their homes. Most had only minimal knowledge of Jewish life and practice. Yet each possessed a skill that I needed. I asked them to volunteer, to take a chance. They accepted.

My meetings with these prospective teachers followed a pattern. Each was extremely flattered that I had taken the time to ask if I could be invited to their home to discuss a subject of importance. All were slightly nervous, because I had refused to explain over the phone why I wanted to visit. Every one of them flushed and hesitated to respond when I told them that I thought they were good communicators with skills and enthusiasm that could motivate young students from elementary school age through high school and that the community needed their talents. Finally, each agreed to take on the task because I was willing to take the risk along with them.

Leonard was correct. On some level each of these people believed that our product, Judaism, if properly taught, could make a difference. Once they overcame their initial fears, they were willing to take a risk because they believed in the product. They stepped forward to interact with Judaism in a new and exciting manner. Years after I left that community, I learned that most of them continued to serve as volunteer teachers. A few ascended the congregational hierarchy and became synagogue presidents.

These two incidents helped me understand that people come forward to volunteer if they are approached in the right way – that is, if volunteering is marketed to them as a meaningful endeavor.

Unfortunately, too many not-for-profit organizations stumble along in a not-so-happy way, which results in bruised feelings, insensitive responses, and burnout on the part of volunteers and professionals.

In deciphering the cultures of Jewish organizations, the cultural differences cannot be overlooked. Failing to take an organization's culture into account can undermine the entire enterprise. We can never forget that volunteering is a two-way street. Volunteers must be motivated, but volunteer organizations also need to maximize volunteer satisfaction. Blaming one or the other for the failures prevalent today in the world of Jewish volunteerism helps no one. The search is for a win-win strategy.

(*Excerpted from* BUILDING A SUCCESSFUL VOLUNTEER CULTURE, by **Rabbi Charles Simon**, Jewish Lights Publishing, 2009)

JEWISH LEADERSHIP: BIBILICAL & MODERN

(I have had the pleasure of knowing Rabbi Charles Simon since I was in rabbinical school in the mid-1980s. As a supervisor of our national college outreach program, OMETZ, Chuck shared practical wisdom with me while I was its student director. Since then, our friendship has blossomed across the years and decades and we have reflected together on a wide range of issues facing contemporary Jewish life. I offer these thoughts on leadership as a tribute to him and to his leadership, which has been a gift to us all.)

When we think about something as amorphous as "leadership," what exactly are we talking about? At first glance, we might assume that we mean the ability to coerce individuals to do what we want them to do. While forcing an agenda can be a mark of leadership, making a community conform to one's personal desires is sometimes a failure of true leadership, infantilizing the community for the sake of gratifying a frail ego at the top. In fact, leadership is a process, one that enables a community to successfully respond to issues facing its membership. To understand the components of good leadership, it is helpful to distinguish between three different, but related concepts: power, authority, and leadership. [1]

Power is imposed on another person; rather than accepting power as a free offering, it is generally taken. Power is coercive, often having no restraint other than greater power. As much as we might recoil from a frank display of strength, there are times when the appropriate leadership choice is power. A few years ago we witnessed NATO and the allied forces determine (finally) that the situation in the Balkans had become outrageous, and that the Serb leadership seemed deaf to diplomacy, decency, or world opinion. Since the Serbs were relying on brute power to enforce their goals, power seemed to the allies to be the only available response. In our own history, the Philistine occupation of Eretz Yisrael was one of conquest and might. Only the military mobilization of Israel's earliest kings, Saul and David, was able to achieve the dual goals of security and integrity. One of the fundamental realities of national and international conflict is that power is sometimes the only option available to enable a community to continue as a community, and to be able to move forward.

---

[1] Much of this analysis is based on Ronald Heifetz, <u>Leadership without Simple Answers</u> (Cambridge: Harvard University Press, 1996.)

But power has its price. The problem with power is that it undermines a more basic kind of leadership, that of authority. Authority, unlike power, is never imposed. It is always conferred. It is always given. For example, I am a rabbi. I have no power, only the authority you are willing to extend to my words. The minute I say something so outrageous that I have deeply offended my listeners, they respond by no longer listening, and there is nothing I may do to bring them back. Jewish leadership — rabbinic and lay — is under the guise of authority because our communities are completely voluntaristic. No one has to join, no one has to remain a member, and each individual selects involvement at the level (and frequency) he or she desires at the time.

Power and authority often work at cross-purposes. If I am someone who has authority I can selectively invoke power, but every time I do that I use up some of my authority, and ultimately wind up having none left. So it is true that as a rabbi in a congregation I can announce to my congregation that if they do not follow this policy which I feel is fundamentally important I am going to quit. But a rabbi only gets to say that once, twice at the most, and then everyone on the Board responds to that threat with "Rabbi, be our guest." So the notion that all leadership involves power is false. To the contrary, power can corrode authority.

Look, for example, in this century at the former Soviet Union, it should rest in peace. The Soviet Union was an empire based almost exclusively on power with virtually no authority. The Czech people did not confer their leadership on the Soviets. The Soviets took it. And one of the things that that meant was that the moment the Soviet Union was no longer able to mobilize power (meaning the ability to impose its will on subjugated peoples) it simply dissolved. It had no residual authority left. No one followed Soviet dictate simply because the Kremlin provided authority, because they felt it was right, but because they felt connected to it. That distinction I think is important to us to remember as leaders in the Jewish community, because the Jewish community, particularly in the United States, is an exclusively voluntary association. None of you have to attend Jewish lectures, and no Jew has to be a Jew! I am not talking at the level of theology — whether God thinks you have to be a Jew. That I leave to you and your conscience and your rabbis. But as a matter of sociology, we live in a remarkable country. We live in a place and time in which we are perfectly free to say, "I'm not interested in any connection to the Jewish community whatsoever. I am not interested in religion, I am not interested in the ethnicity, and I don't need the Federation." The world out there has no trouble with the choice to opt out. The world outside, if anything, encourages the choice of abandoning our particular identity and just melting into the general American mix. So, in our age, any Jew who participates in communal life is someone who chooses to be part of the Jewish community as opposed to someone who is forced to participate. We have no power in the Jewish community. We have only authority. That constraint is true for rabbis, for the Federation, and for lay leadership, now and in the future.

In that regard we need to think about leadership as a trust. Leadership is a dynamic relationship between the leader and the community, between the leaders and the followers. Leadership, above all else, is an activity. It is not simply attaining a goal; it is the process of mobilizing followers to address their own needs. Leadership is not about successfully imposing a particular outcome. That is not real leadership – that's power! Leadership is the ability to say to a group – look at the issues that our community needs to address, now let's move forward on the issues.

Helping a community muster a response to an issue can lead to very different responses. Sometimes what a community needs to do is push ahead even though an issue is very disruptive. Sometimes addressing an issue prematurely will destroy the community. So sometimes a mark of great leadership is the ability to distract individuals so that they don't notice the issue until they are finally ready as a community to confront it and to resolve it in a positive way. Leadership doesn't always mean pushing ahead. Sometimes a good leader is one who knows when to dodge an issue. At the beginning of President Clinton's administration the first issue that got put on his docket was an issue that nobody had wanted there: gays in the military. People who were antigay didn't want it because they didn't want gays in the military, while people who were pro-gay didn't want it because frankly that is not the first issue with which gays and lesbians were wrestling. Somehow it got shoved on the docket and an inability to lead surfaced in the administration's failure to control the agenda. It was selected for them. One of the things you need to be aware of as individuals leading the Jewish community is being able to know when it is the right time to raise an issue, and how far to go with that issue. As with so much in life, in the leadership business, timing is everything.

Leadership, I believe, has to be transformational. If your community is no different because of your leadership, then you are not really leading. Therefore, with regard to my last general observation, leadership always requires a commitment to values. There is no value neutral way to lead. To be a leader means being able to help a community transform itself. To be able to mobilize individuals and work in a partnership with them, relying on authority rather than on power, requires having a clear sense of values which are shared between the leaders and the community. It is by negotiating those shared values that the leader in the community is able to help sift out which issues need to be addressed at a given time and which issues need to be put aside for a while.

To recapitulate: Authority, leadership, and power are three distinct concepts. Leadership is an activity, not the ability to impose an agenda or an outcome. In our time, Jewish leadership relies exclusively on authority and almost never on power.

When I look at Biblical models of leadership and authority the first one who comes to mind is our father Abraham. Abraham is a remarkable leader because he has absolutely no power. He is just the head of the family, and all he has is this meshugeneh idea that God wants something from him. What is remarkable about Abraham in terms of leadership is his ability to mobilize his entire family around a shared value, a key idea. He does it because of his charisma, because of the force of the idea. Think about it: Abraham is able to get his clan to go on a journey where nobody even knows the destination. That is especially remarkable because I imagine all of you have been in the position where you have tried to persuade your family to go somewhere where you did know where the destination was and that, in itself, is already pretty tough. Try getting a Jewish family to go somewhere simply on faith: "I'll tell you where we are going once we're going." Our entire people's history is based on that kind of faith and that kind of leadership, on the ability to look to Abraham and walk on his journey without knowing where we are headed.

The other piece that I get from Abraham is actually a negative piece. Abraham is a leader who puts public leadership above all else in his life. He kicks out one son because the voice he hears tells him to do that. He puts another son on the sacrificial altar and almost kills him. When Abraham returns his wife is dead possibly because of that, and the Torah doesn't mention either of his sons ever speaking to him again. His last recorded conversation with Isaac is while they are still walking to the Akedah.

So part of what we need to consider with Abraham as a model of leadership is: to what extent does leadership involve necessarily abandoning the people you love? Part of the challenge for our generation is that we are really the first generation to refuse to make that choice by-and-large. In other words both men and women in our generation insist on a career, while also being active spouses and active parents. But Abraham is a warning to us that sometimes public leadership requires sacrificing family and this reality is something to be on guard against, or at least something of which we must be aware.

My second inspirational leader in Genesis is Sarah. Abraham, after all, is the one who heard the voice. So it is relatively easy for him to decide to give everything up and boldly go where no Jew had gone before. But Sarah hears nothing except her husband's enthusiasm, and she is willing to make his passion her own. To my mind that makes her a great leader in her family. Now by that I don't mean simply the "stand by your man" routine. I mean that to be a leader (recall our insistence on shared values) one prominent value surely has to be allowing the community to flower in its own way. One's leadership can't be too agenda driven. It can't be so specific that we fail to listen to the passions of the people we are seeking to lead. That principal is certainly true in the world of the UJC/Federations. Our leadership is a leadership of service and of caring. It simply will not do for those of us who are active to insist, "Here is what we are willing to provide – now take it." Instead what we have to do is mobilize our communal resources and then listen to our community, so that when it comes to us and says, "Here is what the need is" we may help facilitate the attainment of that goal. Sarah is a remarkable giant of spirit in her willingness to nurture Abraham's passion and allow it to achieve fruition.

The next great hero, and one who is often overlooked, is Isaac. Isaac is the least famous of the patriarchs, perhaps because of the choices that he makes in his life. Abraham — Isaac's father — is certainly known because he is the one who started our relationship with God. Jacob — Isaac's son — is well-known because he is the ancestor of all the Jewish people, and we are known by his name, Israel. Isaac, let's be frank, is a nebbish. He is the middle guy, not as great as his dad is, not as great as his son. Let's take a few moments to rally on behalf of the lesser-known guys in the middle.

In a world in which change can seem the ultimate value, being able to know what to hold on to, what to abandon, and what to transmit is a great act of leadership. If everything changes, then no one can ever talk to anyone else. Every generation is alienated from the generations before it and can never gain access to inherited wisdom or insight. Somebody has got to be willing to take seriously what he or she has inherited from the past, to sift through it and say, "Here is what can still speak in our time." Isaac is precisely that patriarch.

Of all the patriarchs, Isaac is the only one who never leaves the land of Israel. Abraham leaves because of a famine, Jacob leaves because of a famine, and Isaac would rather starve in his homeland than abandon what he has inherited and what he must transmit. Of the patriarchs, there is only one of whom it is said that he and his wife love each other. Of all the figures in the Bible, only of Isaac is it said that he loves Rebecca and she loves him. We don't hear of love between Abraham and Sarah. We know that Jacob loves (or at least lusts for) Rachel, but we never learn of her feelings for him. David, that great romantic, goes after Bathsheba (and many other women in his day) but we never learn of his emotional attachment, nor of theirs. Alone of all the Bible's figures, only Isaac and his wife explicitly enjoy a relationship of mutual love. Perhaps that is why, when his wife is barren, Isaac is the only husband who prays on her behalf without having to be told to do that, because Isaac knows that if Rebecca has a problem then they both have a problem.

I think Isaac gleaned that insight during the Akedah. Anyone who has ever suffered a life-threatening experience knows that it radically transforms your priorities. From that moment on you are acutely aware that life is a gift, that life is precious, and that we generally squander that gift because we mistakenly think there will always be more time. Isaac came up against that knife, and he knew that there might not be any more time. The recognition that time is fleeting and precious means we reprioritize and focus on what matters most in life. As for the rest, we learn to let go. That might be the very reason why Isaac is the least famous of the patriarchs, and the one who had a decent marriage.

His wife is also a remarkable woman. In an age in which women were largely viewed as adornments to their husbands, Rebecca is the Bible's first feminist. Rebecca, unlike all the other ladies of the Torah who wait passively by the well for some big strong strapping man to feed the herd, moves the stone and handles it herself, thank you very much. She is, of all the matriarchs, the one who rules her family. It is clear throughout their lives that her husband Isaac keeps misreading their boys, and she keeps making the right call. Isaac picks the son who should not inherit the covenant; Rebecca selects the one who should. Indeed, let's note that God works through her and not through Isaac. She is the one that makes sure that Jacob inherits the birthright. She is the one who makes sure he escapes in time to not get murdered by Esau, and it is her vision and her strength that enables us to have a forefather in Jacob.

What I learn from Rebecca is that leadership sometimes requires breaking the mold. It isn't always sufficient for a leader simply to meet expectations. That kind of leadership quickly devolves into pandering. Sometimes a leader has to create the expectations and leave it to individuals afterwards to realize that that wasn't so unreasonable a stance after all.

Then there's Jacob, everyone's favorite patriarch. What I learn from Jacob is that you are not doomed to be who you always were. Jacob, frankly, is really annoying as a kid. He is driven by ambition, he is wily, and he is somewhat unscrupulous. He is mean to his big dumb brother and, by-and-large, a questionable ancestor for a holy people. What is remarkable about Jacob is that he learns from life. He, of all the patriarchs, suffers the most. When he is finally brought down in front of Pharaoh he says that his days are shorter than the days of his father and his grandfather and have been full of sorrow. He is the one who fell passionately in love with Rachel and then ending up marrying her sister by mistake. Jacob is the one whose beloved wife can't have children. Every time he turns around Leah has another child. He doesn't care; he only has eyes for Rachel. While the Torah nowhere says that she loved him, he is clearly infatuated with her. When she finally does bear a first child, Jacob adores that child above all others. Rachel has a second child and dies in childbirth so that Jacob doesn't get to live further with the woman with whom he was passionately in love. Then he is led to believe that the son that he favors above all his other children has been killed by a wild animal. Thus he spends much of his life mourning the loss of both Rachel and Joseph. As if that were not enough, along comes the terrible famine whereupon he is told that the Pharaoh wants the only other remaining child of his dear Rachel. This is a guy who knows suffering and hardship, and this is a guy who grows to be the Bible's greatest figure other than Moses.

Jacob by the middle of his life has become a true father to us all and a spiritual giant. Life brings pain. A great leader, I believe, is one who doesn't flee from the pain but who learns from it, and who allows whatever life brings to be a teacher. We cannot chose what life will bring us, but we can choose how we respond to what life brings.

The last leader I want to mention is Moses, a fascinating character because he grows up not knowing who he really is. He grows up in an Egyptian court and then at some point feels a strong infinity for the Hebrew slaves. We don't know whether that is because he is a Hebrew or because he is just a sensitive person, and rabbinic legend has it both ways.

What I think is extraordinary about the leadership of Moses is that he understands that ethics and ritual can never be separate, and that a religion that is only concerned with ritual is idolatrous and a religion only concerned with ethics sinks ultimately into mere lip service. If all we are doing is talking the talk, our chatter will not last long, and it certainly won't repair the world. There has to be ways to constantly reinforce the ethical imperatives at the core of our sacred traditions. Moses' religion is the only one I know of where the most frequently mentioned commandment is that there should be one law alike for the Israelite and for the stranger who is in our midst. The insight that all people are made in God's image, and translating that radical insight into law, is something that we continually strive to understand and for which each generation continues to uncover new implications and applications. We used to think that principle only meant white men, and then we realized that it also meant people of color. In our age we started to realize that it includes women, and gays, and those with special needs, and those not-yet with special needs. As the franchise expands, we keep looking at Moses' precedent and seeing in it a circle that gets continually bigger and bigger. Either everybody is made in God's image or there is no God worth serving.

Moses is someone who put his passion for social justice at the center of his leadership, and in everything he does demonstrates that you can't be indifferent to other human beings and still remain a Jewish leader. Indeed, you can't be indifferent to human beings and be a Jew. That, I believe, is the legacy of the leadership of Moses.

Notice also that Moses lacks personal grace. He is a rotten speaker; he says so himself. Although, frankly, I have to say that I think his Book of

Deuteronomy is a fairly good speech. Moses doesn't have committees helping him with anything. He doesn't have organizational skills. His father-in-law has to come in and help him organize the office. Yet, lacking all of those accoutrements and lacking power, what he had was authority. The Jewish people looked to him and continue to look to him as a leader. Without power he took his authority and brought his people to the borders of the Promised Land.

And so must we.

Rabbi Dr. Bradley Shavit Artson (www.bradartson.com) holds the Abner and Roslyn Goldstine Dean's Chair of the Ziegler School of Rabbinic Studies and is Vice President of American Jewish University in Los Angeles. He supervises the Miller Introduction to Judaism Program and mentors Camp Ramah in California (Ojai) and Camp Ramah of Northern California (Monterey Bay). He is also dean of the Zacharias Frankel College in Potsdam, Germany, ordaining Conservative rabbis for Europe. He is the author of 12 books and over 250 articles, most recently Renewing the Process of Creation: A Jewish Integration of Science and Spirit (Jewish Lights).

CREATING A RUACH CULTURE

Some twenty-five years ago, I was invited to attend a reunion dinner of the attendees of the New England Region's annual retreat. My sponsor and I got tied up in Boston traffic. We arrived late to the dinner. We entered the front door of the catering hall and came upon some forty men in the middle of *benching*. It was a thrilling sight to behold. A short, delightful gentleman (Sam Primack of blessed memory) was leading the group. He and the gathering were all smiles, filled with joy and mostly, especially, *ruach*. Witnessing this event profoundly changed my life.

When the FJMC asked me to lead the way to invigorate a ritual practice that could be taught and shared with all of our clubs, the *benching* of the *Birkat Hamazon* (the blessings after a meal), became our focus. Instead of something being mumbled through if done at all, we would turn it into a vigorous and joyful group effort. We would teach them how to do it with ruach.

The word *ruach* commonly means wind, breath, or spirit, and its roots are found in the beginning of Genesis, chapter 1:

1) When God began to create the heaven and the earth —

2) The earth being unformed and void, with darkness over the surface of the deep and a wind (*v'roo-ach*) from God sweeping over the water,

3) God said, "Let there be light;" and there was light.

Light is always positive in Torah and a simple reading implied by the proximity of these few but powerful words teaches us that when we mirror and multiply God's spirit with our own breath and voice we can take moments and make them holy and filled with light. *Kol vachomer* – all the more so – if we can infuse our prayers and our moments for blessing with *ruach* – with God's spirit – we will be led to even more light as well; light that can infuse and shine upon our meetings, deliberations or whatever follows our moment of *ruach*.

We began to train people to lead the *benching* which begins with simple responses and built into group singing. At the New England Region retreat, where I had the privilege of being master of ceremonies for several years, I saw that once we unleashed this spirit, this *ruach*, there was no holding back. Men began to rhythmically bang on the tables and by the time we finished there was no desire to stop, continuing an extra verse as a *niggun*, a wordless melody.

At our conventions, with hundreds of men (and many wives) in attendance, the celebration of our meals together continued to build. Men would stand at the end and wave their napkins. At a subsequent convention they were issued *shmattas* – dubbed "*ruach* rags" – which were color-coded by region. At the end of a heartfelt *Birkat* the room erupted into a sea of waving cloths, embracing both the gratitude for a good meal and a celebration of Brotherhood.

It isn't unusual for those who witness the full expression of Brotherhood ruach for the first time to be taken aback, or to misinterpret the sheer volume of sound that typically goes along with it, as just being loud for the sake of being loud. They might suggest it is behavior more appropriate to USY or other youth groups. But they soon come to realize, as so many before them have, that reaching up to God with honest energy and exuberance is an experience that is open to any soul and certainly has no age limit.

How do you bring the power of *ruach* into your club and into your shul? *Benching* is a relatively easy, but specific way to begin. The first step would be to get a recording of a spirited rendition of benching and also printed booklets of the text, known as *Benchers*. Then get together a core group of men to learn the ritual and practice, practice, practice. And, if possible, find one man with a good voice to serve as leader. Go at the whole thing with the thought that you want to bring something bold and beautiful into the community. When your *ruach* group is ready, introduce it at the next men's club or synagogue event. If you go about it right, the delivery of *benching* properly executed will not only be effective but lots of fun as well. Go from practice sessions into using your group's expertise in *benching* with *ruach* and then extend this into other areas of ritual as well.

When you get into this project, inevitably you will discover energy and enthusiasm amongst your members that you never imagined was there. This in turn can lead to camaraderie and a degree of teamwork that has the potential to raise the level of whatever activity or program you and your club may choose to do. Indeed, you just may find that *ruach*, and the spirit it fills you with, is worth pursuing as a beautiful thing in itself.

Burton L. Fischman, PhD., has earned the nickname "Captain Ruach" for his spirited leading of benching at the FJMC's biennial conventions. Now in his 80s, he continues his work in training and inspiring the FJMC leaders of tomorrow.

THE OFFICAL® HISTORY OF
THE INTERNATIONAL KIDDUSH CLUB

It's unusual for a rabbi to be involved in a Kiddush club.

Yet from the beginning of the International Kiddush Club (IKC), which convenes every two years at the FJMC's biennial convention, we had the blessing of Rabbi Simon (or Chuck, as we call him) who understood the need to channel the leadership skills of a few of the FJMC members and to act "outside of the box." The use of a group outside of the normal stream and programs at convention was a unique opportunity to engage men (and women!) in activities that have enhanced the FJMC and its leadership in the Conservative/Masorti world who might otherwise not have been excited about the opportunities offered.

There have been Kiddush clubs in *shuls* for as long as there have been *shuls*. Making a *"l'chaim"* after *davening* is one of the unique aspects of Judaism; our belief that the mundane parts of life can be elevated to a higher status through prayer is one of the central parts of our faith. We eat, sleep, and drink, etc. with a blessing. The blessing makes the action holy, not just through making it, but also through the reflection one gets from pausing before the act to stop and make the blessing. We think about what we are going to do and we have the intention to perform the act after a religious moment. We bring holiness to these acts through the blessing, through the thought that goes into it and through our commitment.

This is not to suggest that either the FJMC or the IKC is all about alcohol, but that we include all aspects of life in our practice of Judaism. There is no prohibition on alcoholic beverages in moderation. In fact, one of our most important and sacred acts is to consecrate Shabbat and holidays with the Kiddush (blessing) over wine. If proper wine is not available, any kosher alcohol or juice may be substituted. It's not about the drink, it's about the Kiddush.

The story of the IKC began in July 2001, when the FJMC held its first weekend convention in Toronto, Canada. Previously the conventions had taken place in Catskill and Poconos resorts and went from Sunday to Thursday. The 2001 convention began on Wednesday and ended on Sunday, so, for the first time Shabbat was part of the convention. This was also the first time that the convention had been held in a city, and the leadership of the FJMC tried very hard to bring some of the customs of the community into the convention. While we toured Toronto and saw the sights, we also participated in the Shabbat tradition of a Kiddush club. It was not a large event; a table at the back of the room where we held services with a few bottles of scotch and some donated herring and crackers, but it began the tradition.

The next convention, through circumstance and the arcane liquor laws of Florida, required us to buy the liquor from the hotel, which required payment and membership to allow the club to continue. We created a ticket system and introduced membership cards and created a leadership structure, in a very FJMC way, innovating and involving more than 100 participants. On Shabbat morning, the hotel bartender arrived, put up his little table and started to convert cards to drinks. It worked out wonderfully. On Saturday night we subtracted the hotel charge from our collection and found that we had turned a "profit" of $1100 which we gave to Chuck for a pet project of his, buying tefillin for Latin American Masorti congregations which could not afford to buy them for themselves. Another tradition was born.

We raised the price to $36.00 for the 2005 convention, also in Florida. We sold just as many "memberships" and raised even more money. We also gave each "member" a shot glass and a lapel pin, which we have continued to do at each FJMC convention. We also began to have a Kiddush Club Oneg Shabbat on Friday night, removing it from Shabbat morning services. This effort raised about $6000 through the sales of the memberships and other items, which went straight to the Tefillin Fund.

FJMC convened in Chicago in 2007 and the IKC raised the price again. Once again we held the event on Friday night where we were joined by Chazzanim Alberto Mizrachi, Steven Stoehr and David Propis, all of whom were totally ready on Shabbat morning. It might seem surprising to non-members, but that's something we stress: IKC members are always first in the room for services. In 2009, we had over 160 members in Philadelphia over the July 4th weekend. This time we priced the membership at $39.99. We held the IKC meeting on the 33rd floor of the Loew's hotel and had a fantastic view of the fireworks on three sides. Another $7000 was raised. The tradition continued two years later when we raised more than that in California.

Since we meet now on Friday night after the end of regular programing, our "meeting" consists of telling a few stories, having a few *l'chaims*, and then on to bed. But we added a few new things in California. A couple of our members had lost family members and, as mourners, were not supposed to attend large gatherings during their year of saying *Kaddish*. There are a few exceptions to the rule, however, and one is for attendance at study and a siyum on the conclusion of a chapter of Talmud. So if we completed a chapter, everyone there would be able to join in the siyum, and nobody would be excluded from the event.

Masechet Magillah was being studied by a few of our leaders and, planners that we are, the last few lines were all that were left to study. And if you complete the end of the chapter, you get credit for the whole chapter. Copies were made and brought to the patio for our 11:30 p.m. event, and before a drop was poured, out came the copies and the last few lines were read and explained. We all then said *Kaddish d'rabbanan* (the Rabbi's Kaddish, traditionally said after study) and made our *l'chaims*. As it happens, we didn't tell our Rabbi Simon about our plans. Along with some special guests who had never been to our event, he walked out the door onto the patio as 40 people were chanting *Kaddish*. He picked up on our plans right away, denied prior knowledge when asked, and explained that we often do things like this, surprising even him.

We continued to discuss Torah, Talmud and the origins of Scotch whisky well into the night. And since most of us were still on Eastern or Central time, it was a very late night. Yet we were all there for the opening *"baruch"* at *Shacharit* the next morning, and some of us even helped make a special *hashkama* (early) minyan with the mashgiach (supervisor of *kashruth*) who was saying *Kaddish* at 7:30 a.m.!

We had a great time, but it didn't end there. In 2012, the FJMC sponsored a trip to South America which included a visit to the shul in Iquitos, Peru, a town that literally has no road access to the outside world. Rabbi Simon and the group travelling with him brought mezuzot and tefillin to the Jews there, something that many had never dreamed of owning, financed in part by the IKC.

The tradition continued in 2013, with another great convention north of Boston. Over 200 people joined the club and gathered and celebrated until way, way too late. Yet they ALL made it to services the next morning, as they always do. We had another great group of *chazzanim* with us and as you can see from the YouTube videos that are scattered around the internet, we all had a great time, again!

So, yes, the IKC has more than proven itself as a place for Jewish brotherhood and celebration and for supporting our brethren around the world. Yet what about inspiring men's club leadership? The 2015 convention was special for a number of reasons. First, we went back to Florida, where the IKC was really formed. Second, Allan Gottesman, one of IKC's founders, was installed as the president of the FJMC. 2017 will be bittersweet with Rabbi Simon's retirement, yet it will also mark the ascension of another of our founders, Stan Greenspan, as president of the FJMC. Looking ahead to 2019, a third founder, Tom Sudow, is set to succeed Stan.

What began as a lark has become one of the more unusual FJMC initiatives yet one that continues to have an impact both within the organization and in the greater Jewish world. In early 2017, the FJMC conducted its first mission to Jewish community in Cuba and the IKC made sure there were funds to give every Jewish household on that island a mezuzah. We've been able to make many wonderful things happen with the FJMC, bringing our unique "brand" of Judaism to a whole lot more people. We expanded our activities to the World Zionist Congress in 2010 and 2015, setting the stage to have it get better in the years to come.

We continued to support the Tefillin Fund, which now buys mezuzot too, and the total given to the Tefillin Fund by the IKC has exceeded $60,000 to date. The only alcohol we use IKC funds for is at the biennial convention. All other meetings or events that may crop up are hosted out of the goodness of those bringing the drinks. The critics? (There are always critics, it's a Jewish organization!) They like us now. They have seen the *ruach* we bring to the organization and they have all become members!

Through the years, the IKC has had a lot of fun but has also done a lot of good, allowing us to get tefillin and mezuzot to Jewish communities that cannot afford them. It's also involved more Jewish men in Jewish life and that, after all, is what the FJMC is all about.

Stan Greenspan is the incoming president of the FJMC and one of the founders of the IKC.

THE SECRET SAUCE:
FOSTERING A GRASSROOTS STRUCTURE

One of the FJMC's most important values is that, historically, it has always recognized that the strength of our movement was in the local men's club or congregation. This approach significantly differs from the way most organizations act when they wish to enrich and build up a community. The general assumption for most groups is a top down approach, with the answer to most challenges being to bring in additional professionals. FJMC's attitude differs because we have always posited that if one wishes to strengthen a community one must empower those who have the most at stake: those who live there.

Given that underlying premise, the FJMC leadership realized that if we wished to maintain local allegiance from our clubs it was necessary to create a variety of vehicles that would deliver service. Service was defined as being both programmatic (Yom HaShoah candles, Worldwide Wrap, Hearing Men's Voices – i.e., programs developed by the FJMC) and hands-on (sending trained volunteers to assist clubs facing challenges). The goal was always to increase volunteer engagement at the local level.

In order to be able to deliver both programmatic and hands-on service FJMC organized itself by Regions. One of the primary functions of a Region was to bring club leadership together to exchange ideas and learn from one another. In order to further strengthen the ties between the individual club and its Region, FJMC encouraged each Regions to create their own regional identities and activities. Regional identities were fostered, for example, by the introduction of a regional kippah. Regional kippot were sported at regional events, such as Man of the Year and Youth of the Year brunches or dinners. These events created regional awareness and, with a bit of encouragement, would lead regional leadership to develop their own regional projects. Regional projects have included activities like concerts, walkathons and bike-a-thons, which raised funds for the local club and for a regional project such as their local Camp Ramah. As a result of these efforts, these Conservative summer camps are currently being supported by seven FJMC Regions with the added benefit that the fathers of some of our campers are attracted to support their own Men's Club or Brotherhoods.

The grassroots structure is further supported programmatically as the Regions and the International encourage their affiliates to apply for Torch and Quality Club Awards. Torch Award and the Quality Club Award recipients are named every two years at the FJMC biennial convention. The Torch Awards reflect the clubs' most successful and innovative programmatic efforts for their synagogue. The sharing of the knowledge of these programs reflect FJMC at its best. These awards are one of the ways that FJMC guides its clubs into specific areas which reflect the FJMC's and the Movement's agenda. The programs that are awarded have been written up in detail and that information is then disseminated to all affiliates. This further connects them to their Region and to the International organization by giving them fresh ideas that can be adapted to local needs and interests.   As is evidenced by this volume, many of FJMC's signature initiatives began with a program at a local club that was then allowed to grow and evolve. The "secret sauce" of the FJMC's recipe for success is no secret at all. It is encouraging and recognizing innovation at the local level, and then sharing it with all our members, strengthening the organization and the Conservative movement as a whole.

Rabbi Charles Simon was the executive director of the FJMC from 1983 to 2017.

THE INITIATIVES:
HOW THE FJMC HAS MADE A DIFFERENCE

For nearly four decades the FJMC has been introducing new initiatives to fulfill their goal of "helping Jewish men lead Jewish lives." Although the resulting programs have varied in subject matter and format, they share a common pattern: a club or region comes up with an idea, it is expanded upon and broadcast by the FJMC leadership, and it goes back to the local level, where it has an impact on individuals, clubs, and congregations. The result of these activities have had the effect of changing the conversation for the movement as a whole.

IT STARTS WITH HEBREW LITERACY

In 1963 Rabbi Noah Golinkin, then based in Arlington, Virginia, embarked on a simple initiative that would – in partnership with the Federation of Jewish Men's Clubs – transform the Conservative movement. Many congregants were struggling with prayers in Hebrew, if they could read them at all. At a time when what our tradition calls *Lashon HaKodesh* (the Holy Tongue) had been brought back to life in modern Israel, American Jews were losing their connection to the language of our tradition, one that had historically bound together Jews from all over the world.

Rabbi Golinkin began a program at his synagogue to teach his congregants how to read Hebrew. He had two innovations, both of which would prove fruitful. First, laypeople would teach laypeople. This had the effect of allowing the adult students to feel they were learning with peers rather than with someone who might – in reality or not – take a dim view of their ignorance of the language. Second, multiple classes were offered at a variety of times, recognizing that for this project to work it had to accommodate the schedules of the students, and not the other way around.

In 1978, Rabbi Golinkin, in conjunction with FJMC, published <u>Shalom Aleichem</u>. It was a co-venture of FJMC and Hebrew Publishing Company, marking FJMC's first foray into creating books for the Jewish community. It would not be the last. The book taught the letters and vowels, and combined them into the words of the prayer book for the Friday night Shabbat service. This was about becoming engaged with the synagogue service, not learning how to order off a menu in Tel Aviv. The idea spread and the FJMC saw this as an initiative that was both innovative and would serve the needs of its members. Daniel Stern, past international FJMC president, recalls:

> I was on the board of my men's club when... our club decided to participate in the project and I was selected to chair the program. I solicited instructors from the congregation (about 10) and we advertised that we would be running a program to teach congregants how to read Hebrew...

> Since Rabbi Golinkin was serving Beth Shalom Congregation in Columbia, Maryland at the time (less than one half hour from our synagogue), we invited him to train our instructors at our initial

meeting. The session went very well and we were able recruit about 60 students who wanted to learn to read Hebrew... I conducted two more classroom sessions a few years later and I ran the classes myself. In all, we taught over 100 students how to read Hebrew.

Stern's experience was replicated across the U.S. and Canada. The FJMC enthusiastically sponsored the Hebrew literacy initiative, helping clubs across North America obtain the materials needed for peer-to-peer learning. In 1981 Rabbi Golinkin published a follow-up to his book with a second volume, <u>Ayn Keloheynu</u>, where the focus now was not merely reading Hebrew, but comprehending the Shabbat morning service.

Rabbi Golinkin's books were crucial elements of the campaign, but it's unlikely that it would have enjoyed the success it did without the full backing of the FJMC which created two support guides showing clubs how to set up the program and volunteer teachers how to run their classes. The "Implementation Guide" and the "Teacher's Guide" made sure that the clubs were working with a net and didn't have to stumble around wondering what to do next.

The rest of the Conservative movement took notice. Dr. Gerson D. Cohen, then chancellor of the Jewish Theological Seminary of America, wrote the introduction to the original "Implementation Guide," praising the FJMC initiative:

> It's commendable purpose is to make Hebrew, the classic and eternal vehicle of our religious self-expression, accessible to every man, woman, and child in our communities. In implementing this program, the Federation has in effect become a surrogate parent, enabling every congregant to participate intelligently and with a full heart in the synagogue service or in home worship.

In 1992 the Rabbinical Assembly (RA) proclaimed 1992-2002 the "Decade of Hebrew Literacy." Rabbi Allan Silverstein, then president of the RA, announced in 1995 that they would be partnering with the FJMC on the Hebrew Literacy campaign. It is estimated that some 200,000 new Hebrew readers were created in the U.S. and Canada as a result of the FJMC spearheading this initiative. Although Rabbi Golinkin's books are now out of print, clubs are directed to used book sites to get them or to look for other resources.

The success of this initiative begun some forty years ago is still felt today, not only in the number of people who have learned to participate and follow services, but by opening the door for other FJMC projects such as "The Art of Jewish Living."

Daniel M. Kimmel is the editor of this *Festschrift*.

FROM THE RECORD

IT STARTS WITH HEBREW LITERACY

FROM THE FORWARD TO SHALOM ALEICHEM

We fervently hope that every Jewish facility and program will place literacy at the top of their agenda. If we can read the language of our people, we will remain a people, indeed we will remain – as some have termed us – the People of the Book.

Rabbi Charles Simon

FROM THE PREFACE TO SHALOM ALEICHEM

Many of those beginning to learn Hebrew reading will already be familiar with the words of the popular Sabbath eve song, Shalom Aleichem, which this book uses as the basis of its introduction.... As a result, students will learn to read two-thirds of the Hebrew alphabet by the end of Unit 4. Upon completion of Unit 7, they will be able to read the Kiddush, Sh'ma and L'Cha Dodee, as well as Shalom Aleichem itself, and everything else follows!

Rabbi Noah Golinkin

AN INVITATION

We invite you to join us on a voyage of discovery. We shall be searching– for the meaning of words and the meaning behind the words; for the message of the prayers and the story behind the prayers; for the standard formulas of some prayers and for the hidden structures of others.

Start of Unit 1, Ayn Keloheynu

FROM THE OFFICE OF THE CHANCELLOR

The ability to participate in the Sabbath service, for example, should be part of the birthright of every Jew. Such participation entails some facility in Hebrew: the language of the Bible and the prayer book; the sacred tongue of our people, transcending the limitations of time and space. It is the Hebrew language which places American Jews both in the unbroken chain of Jewish history and in the continuum which relates each of us in our communities to our brothers in Israel, and to Jews throughout the modern world.

From the preface to the original "Implementation Guide," Dr. Gerson D. Cohen

DEAR COLLEAGUE

Jewry of the 1990s has the highest level of secular education of any generation of Jews in our history. Yet a sophisticated Jewish adult who lacks Hebrew literacy will feel permanently estranged from Jewish texts and Jewish settings. He or she may well sabotage efforts to make our sons and daughters more learned. The only viable solution is a broad-based campaign of Hebrew Literacy. Thank God, our colleague Rabbi Noah Golinkin and our Federation of Jewish Men's Clubs have created the materials and techniques for transforming this dream in a reality.

From a letter dated May 1995 from Rabbi Alan Silverstein, President, Rabbinical Assembly

A SERMON ON THE IMPORTANCE OF THE HEBREW LANGUAGE

Our lack of familiarity with Hebrew also poses a more immediate and personal problem. Ignorance of Hebrew impedes our participation in Jewish life. Our services call for davening and active participation, not passivity and silence. Going to shul is not like watching an Italian opera or a Mets game. In shul, we are supposed to participate in the performance. The Hebrew words are the focal point of the service. The central ritual object is a scroll written in Hebrew words. Unlike the Christian Church, we do not emphasize the visual, which is reflected in the architecture and art of the church. Similarly, unlike the Catholic Church, we do not focus on the sense of taste which is represented by the taking of the sacraments. Our focus is the Hebrew word, and if we are not comfortable with Hebrew we will not be comfortable with the service. Sometimes there is a quiet and decorum in this sanctuary that is uncharacteristic of a synagogue. Our shul should be filled with pulsating life during prayer....

I have undertaken this Hebrew literacy campaign once before, and I consider it to be one of the most important things I have done in the rabbinate...

From the 1995-1996 "Implementation Guide," Rabbi Neil Kurshan, Huntington Jewish Center

THE ART OF JEWISH LIVING

When Jules Porter, *alav ha-shalom*, was in line to become the International President of FJMC in 1984, he sought advice from Dr. David Lieber, *z"l* and Dr. David Gordis, then President and Vice President at the University of Judaism (now American Jewish University) in Los Angeles. They sent him to see a young Jewish educator on the faculty who had been talking about the need to build the capacity of families to celebrate Jewish life at home, not just in the synagogue. I will never forget our first conversation.

"What should we teach our men?" he asked.

Without hesitation, I said "Shabbat. How to lead a Shabbat ritual in the home."

I knew how life changing Shabbat dinners were in shaping my own Jewish identity and I sensed this was a skill we were in danger of losing. We kicked around ideas for hours. I suggested we needed more than a simple curriculum; we needed a book, an audio recording of the Shabbat melodies, a leader's guide. I told Jules that we did not need an adult education course *about* Shabbat; we needed to model and equip the guys to *make Shabbes*. And thus, the **Art of Jewish Living** series was born.

With the support of the FJMC board, the University of Judaism, and seed money to begin, I turned to my brilliant colleague, Joel Lurie Grishaver, to help shape a curriculum that not only taught the whys and how-to's of the ritual, but one that was illustrated with the stories from real families and individuals who shared their experiences with learning and doing *Shabbes*. I mean, really illustrated…with photos. How fortunate we were that Jules himself was the preeminent social photographer in Los Angeles! And so, we identified people who were eager to share their journeys into Jewish practice. Jules was so excited with this concept that he visited with Jack Roth, a well-respected Jewish bookseller in Los Angeles.

"Could we publish a book of these instructions and interviews? Perhaps I could photograph the people doing *Shabbes* (all photographs will be staged on weekdays, of course) to show the reader exactly what to do." When Jack endorsed the idea, Jules then asked, "How many copies should we print?"

Jack immediately answered, "Well, a Jewish bestseller is 3,000 copies."

Jules was shocked. "We are the 'people of the book' and a bestseller is only 3,000 copies? I can get 3,000 copies just to the guys in our clubs. And I think the book will find an audience in the broader community."

Jack shook his head. "Maybe, but I wouldn't count on it."

And, so, in a purely audacious (read "chutzpahdik") move, Jules set about photographing the families and individuals we interviewed for what was to become **The Art of Jewish Living:** The Shabbat Seder.

After it was published I came to the FJMC convention in the beautiful, dilapidated Concord Hotel in the Catskill Mountains to show the guys how to celebrate a joyous and meaningful Shabbat Seder. We set up an actual Shabbat dinner table on a stage in a ballroom to model how it was done. Then, I taught the guys how to take it home to their local groups so they could teach each other.

Here's an honest question: did the FJMC have any business publishing a book? Not really. But that hardly deterred them. They published a book whose reach went far beyond the local men's clubs, empowering literally thousands of Jews to "DIY" (do it yourself), well before that phrase became a popular mantra.

The success of the Shabbat Seder led to books and materials on Passover, Hanukkah, and A Time to Mourn, A Time to Comfort – a veritable bookshelf of resources for the most-observed moments of the Jewish calendar and life cycle. Always "one step ahead," the FJMC was committed to tackling the most challenging issues in the Jewish community. By including the voices and the photos of Jews by Choice, of single women, of divorcees, of gays and lesbians, we alerted the Conservative movement to the coming tide of demographic change that we knew would inevitably crash into pieces the until-then common depiction of all Jewish families as "nuclear," "intact," and "homogeneous" which appeared in most Jewish books and curricular resources in the movement. We did not shy away from presenting the "December Dilemma" issues with a sensitivity to the complicated emotional dynamic within the extended families of Jews by Choice. While firmly arguing that there was no place for Christmas symbols and celebration within a Jewish home, we recognized that, although the Jew by Choice had converted to Judaism, his or her parents and extended family members had not. Way back in 1990, we anticipated that many Jews would be "visiting" Christmas celebration at the homes of Christian extended family members. We made the distinction between appreciating another religion – even the religion of a close family member – and appropriating it for oneself. In 1995, as the AIDS epidemic swept across North America, we included in <u>A Time to Mourn, A Time to Comfort</u> heart-wrenching pleas from lay and rabbinic leaders of the gay community for support and understanding in the synagogue community and in families as they grappled with the untimely and horrible deaths of gay friends, partners and relatives. This was groundbreaking, not only for the Conservative movement, but for the entire Jewish community.

The **Art of Jewish Living** series was also in the forefront of the nascent efforts to put Jewish family education high on the communal agenda. It was the 1990 National Jewish Population Survey that alarmed the Jewish community and ignited calls for programs of "Jewish continuity." For nearly a decade, a few colleagues had joined me in arguing that families had become far too dependent on the synagogue social hall as the "place" where Shabbat dinners and other celebrations were happening rather than their own dining and living rooms. For those of us involved in creating the emerging field of Jewish family education, the **Art of Jewish Living** books and materials were extraordinarily useful resources to bring Jewish practice and values into the home. In fact, in what may have been a first in the Jewish community, materials that were sponsored by an arm of the Conservative movement found a receptive audience among Reform and independent clergy and educators.

With the publication of each book, I was invited to the biennial convention to introduce the new release as a foundational curriculum for men's clubs. I seem to recall it was a surprise when I brought to convention my brilliant wife Susie to introduce the FJMC "Passover University," a full-on project to teach local congregations the structure of the Haggadah and creative ideas for Seder celebration using our book and materials. I set up a long rope across a stage in the ballroom upon which to reveal the steps of the Passover Seder as outlined in the book. It looked a little like a word puzzle on the television show "Wheel of Fortune." So, naturally, Susie dressed like Vanna White – in a cocktail gown – even though it was nine o'clock in the morning.

The commitment didn't end simply with the introduction of the new book at the FJMC convention. When the leadership realized that thousands of Jewish immigrants from the former Soviet Union were pouring into

North America, they decided to reach out to these new arrivals. They arranged to translate our Passover book into Russian in order to help them learn the Seder ritual.

Once the Art of Jewish Living had found a widespread audience in local Men's Clubs and beyond, it was decided to accept the invitation of Stuart Matlins, the publisher of Jewish Lights Publishing, to take over the distribution of the books. Stuart was such a fan of the books that he authorized me to write a second edition of each volume. I know Jules would be so proud. Wouldn't he have loved to have called up Jack Roth, our supportive but skeptical bookseller, to tell him that when all the editions and benchers and recordings and workbooks in the Art of Jewish Living series are counted since the project started some thirty-seven years ago, well more than 100,000 copies have found their way into Jewish homes, synagogues and classrooms!

The impact of the **Art of Jewish Living** series has been, by all measures, impressive. Since the publication of The Shabbat Seder in 1985, I have traveled extensively to Jewish communities across the world, teaching and inspiring Jewish practice in workshops and lectures based on these books. Inevitably, people will come up to me with a story of how the **Art of Jewish Living** series impacted their lives. Some have held up a dog-eared copy of the Passover book and said, in some variation, "Every year, I take out this book to prepare for a Seder that engages all of our family and guests, young and old."

A grandmother told me, "Our synagogue men's club sponsored an Art of Jewish Living course that taught me how to bring Shabbat into my family when our kids were young; now they have families of their own and wouldn't miss the opportunity to bless their children – my grandchildren! – on Friday nights."

A young couple in an Introduction to Judaism course said, "Thank you for helping me negotiate the December holidays with our Christian family members."

A chavurah mate said to me through tears: "When Nachum died, we turned to the book on mourning for guidance on what to do, how to grieve."

It is one thing to publish a book; it is quite another when the books are read, Post-it noted, wine-stained, and referred to year after year. The FJMC can be quite proud of this important contribution to Jewish life.

Dr. Ron Wolfson is Fingerhut Professor of Education at American Jewish University.

THE YELLOW CANDLE™: THE IDEA THAT SHAPED HOLOCAUST PROGRAMMING

Our sages teach us that saving a life is like saving the world. What happens when 6,000,000 worlds are extinguished in the blink of God's eye? What can survivors do to repair a fractured covenant? What can be done to replace all of those lost worlds, and to build new ones? The answer is the opposite of extinguishing. It is lighting, the physical act of moving from darkness unto light, with a burning candle.

In the Jewish world, candles have long been used to remember lost ancestors on their yahrzeit, the anniversary of their death. Following the Shoah, this ancient custom was revived and expanded to remember those lost in these nightmare years. Lighting one candle, to preserve one memory, is our way of rekindling the Jewish spirit, and recovering from the darkness.

The idea of a candle is not new. But its application to Shoah remembrance is novel. And without FJMC, the idea would never have gained widespread acceptance. The Yellow Candle, over the past 50 years, has touched the lives of millions of people, Jews and non-Jews alike. More people have been made aware of the Yellow Candle than of any other idea or program in the Conservative/Masorti world movement. This is the story of that very special, unusual, candle.

The impact of FJMC on Shoah remembrance is not widely appreciated. FJMC has been the North American Jewish organization primarily responsible for the continued enhancement of Yom HaShoah awareness both in synagogue communities and in our homes.

In the 1970s, survivors started coalescing in events which came to be known as "gatherings." One such conference was held in 1977, among survivors and liberators of the death camps. Survivors began sharing their stories and concerns. One was a ritual issue concerning how to remember lost victims whose families were entirely wiped out. The idea of lighting a dedicated memorial candle for non-relatives, one candle for one victim, arose from these discussions. The survivors returned to their own communities. The idea of a "non-relative" candle started to proliferate in a number of communities.

FJMC began to recognize programming that promoted Holocaust

education and commemoration in 1974, when the Men's Club of Congregation B'nai Jacob in Jersey City, New Jersey received an award for its Yizkor Memorial Service in memory of Yom HaShoah. The club led the way in staking this out as a significant observance by successfully enlisting both Mayor Paul T. Jordan of Jersey City and New Jersey Governor Brendan Byrne to proclaim a "Day of Remembrance". The service was open to the public and speakers from ADL participated, as did six young adults who lit memorial candles. The following year, the program was shared with the leaders of more than 300 congregations.

It was then that Jacob Birnbaum, a survivor of six concentration camps, became vice president of the brotherhood of Congregation Mishkan Tefila in Chestnut Hill, Massachusetts. He accepted the position on the condition that the club host a Holocaust remembrance program. This was something which was practically unheard of and not part of ordinary synagogue programming in the mid-'70s. The program he helped bring about, dubbed "The Eternal Flame," would go on to receive a Gold Torch Award, which is the highest honor awarded to club programming at FJMC's biennial convention. "The Eternal Flame" would serve as the model for synagogue programming for the next several years, thanks to the efforts of men's clubs across the continent.

For Jacob, the notion that we must never forget became a passion. He helped to launch a project called "Facing History and Ourselves," a curriculum for Holocaust education in public schools. Like many other survivors, Jacob spoke extensively in public schools and at community gatherings. Several years later, he wrote and published I Kept my Promise, a memoir about his war experiences. His book and the continuing efforts of the brotherhood of Mishkan Tefila resulted in their receiving another Torch Award at the 1980 FJMC convention.

This is an excellent and early example of how what would become FJMC's commitment to sharing the success stories of its clubs. By allowing other clubs to not only adapt successful programs developed elsewhere for their own needs but come up with their own innovations, each club had the opportunity to add to the project's richness. In 1981, two events occurred simultaneously that would bring the FJMC's commitment to Holocaust education to a new level, stimulating both congregational and home commemoration. Congregation Ner Tamid in Peabody, Massachusetts transformed the traditional Yahrzeit candle into a yellow Yahrzeit candle decorated with symbols of the Holocaust. They distributed these candles complete with boxes and bags to the four hundred members of their congregation. Included in the mailing was a letter and self-addressed envelope, as well as a meditation to be used when lighting the candle. The community responded with donations and the brotherhood used those funds to purchase books about the Holocaust for the libraries in the communities on the North Shore of Boston.

Meanwhile, in Canada, Congregation Beth Tzedec in Toronto, Ontario adapted an Israeli style candle and distributed it to most of the Toronto Jewish community. They requested that individuals light the candle in their homes and make a donation to the synagogue which in turn would use the funds to underwrite the needs of Syrian Jewry. Both clubs submitted their projects for Torch Award consideration and both received honors at the next FJMC Convention.

It was at this point that the FJMC developed this project for national and international use. Known as the Yellow Candle ™, it became a major FJMC activity complete with a guide as well as supportive educational materials. In 1982, 5,000 people in New England lit Yellow Candles ™. These candles were expanded nationally the following year and 60,000 people participated. Since then, the program was adopted in Canada, and has expanded far beyond Conservative congregations.

In the 1980s, FJMC was able to trademark the term Yellow Candle, along with a distinctive graphic consisting of a Jude star (which Jews were required to wear) and barbed wire. Over the years, the Candle program has grown to include accessories such as white boxes for mailing and shipment, and yellow plastic bags with the *Jude* star emblem on the bag. These are used to hang candles and enclosures on door knobs, when they are delivered by volunteers.

In the late 90s and into the new millennium, the program underwent two more changes. Based on the example of Yad Vashem, the Holocaust memorial and museum in Israel, and the involvement of the greater-Jewish community, other religious streams and secular organizations joined in remembrance encompassed under the motto "Branching Out." Today participation in the Candle program has expanded to not only the

Reform movement, but to churches, military bases, JCC's, Jewish Holocaust Museums, and local Jewish Federations. On average, one hundred and fifty thousand people receive Yellow Candles each year.

The second program change was a return to the original program concept, lighting one candle for one victim. This was described powerfully by the expression, "Light One Candle, Preserve a Memory" ™. Increasingly, many candle programs now include the name of one victim who is memorialized. In England, Arizona and Florida, special emphasis is placed on remembering the lost children. Lighting a candle for a child, with their name, age, and other biographical details in mind seems to be a special mitzvah.

The simple yet symbolically powerful observance continues to expand and capture the imagination of people far beyond the synagogue men's clubs in North America where they began. In 2011, 5,000 candles were shipped to Mumbai and the Jewish community of India hosted its first Yom Ha Shoah commemoration. In 2015, the Catholic Dioceses in Arizona adopted the candle program. In 2016, several groups of Christians for Israel began introducing Yom HaShoah programming into the homes of their members. In 2017, the Masorti community in the United Kingdom distributed 3500 candles in their first year of the program. Candles are also being used in Argentina, and Israel. Parallel to this effort, new programmatic suggestions have been included with the material in order to continue to involve existing and emerging generations. It is a program that continues to evolve.

While other organizations have introduced tools or liturgy to insure that the Holocaust will not be forgotten, one wonders how effective they would have been had it not been for the Federation of Jewish Men's Clubs leading the way and ensuring that we must never forget.

Eric Weis was the Shoah Yellow Candle Chairman for the FJMC 2010-2012, and is former president of the Northern New Jersey Region.

FROM THE RECORD

THE YELLOW CANDLE™:
THE IDEA THAT SHAPED HOLOCAUST PROGRAMMING

SOLEMN CEREMONY RECALLS A NIGHTMARE TIME

During a Monday night service attended by nearly 250 people, six yahrzeit or memorial candles were lit, one for each million that died in the war. At least one memorial candle was lit per hour during the remainder of the reading...

The names being read at the bima or pulpit resulted from letters sent to synagogues throughout the state and Jewish and area newspapers. Many were relatives of those responding to the call for names. Between 11,000 and 14,000 names were contributed along with the names of 50,000 French Jews killed at the Auschwitz concentration camp from the Simon Wiesenthal Center in Los Angeles.

From an article by Jeffrey Remz in the Salem, Mass., Evening News, May 7, 1986

YOM-HASHOAH – A DAY FOR ZACHOR, REMEMBRANCE!

The Brotherhood of Temple Ner Tamid will deliver a special Yahrzeit candle to your home within the next few weeks. We ask that you join us on the evening of April 13th, erev Yom-HaShoah, by lighting this Yahrzeit candle in memory of the six million victims of the Holocaust. Place this candle in your window to remind our children and others that the Holocaust DID happen. If we forget, it could happen again.

We would like this to be an annual event on the North Shore; an event that hopefully will spread throughout the region and the country. The cost of the program this year was borne by the Winokur family in memory of Wolfe Winokur... We have a limited supply of extra candles which we will be happy to supply to you for use by relatives and friends who are not included in the Ner Tamid Family...

From a letter dated March 1988 from the Brotherhood of Temple Ner Tamid

YOM HASHOAH YELLOW YAHRZEIT CANDLE PROGRAM 1988

The yellow Yom HaShoah memorial candle designed in 1985 has grown in distribution from 1,200 in the Peabody-Salem, Mass. area in 1986 to 12,000 candles in New England in 1987, through the New England Region FJMC. In 1988, it became a Federation sponsored program, and to date, 48,000 candles have been distributed.

Ninety-five percent of all clubs who ran with this program have favorable remarks and will probably go with the program again for 1989. I was also told that 4-7 clubs in New York and New Jersey that do not belong to the Federation that ran the program, and are now considering joining the Federation...

From a 1988 memo from Joseph Winokur, chairman of the program

AN INTRODUCTION TO THE FEDERATION OF JEWISH MEN'S CLUBS' YOM HASHOA CANDLE PROGRAM

Rabbi Ben Zion Bergman of the Rabbinical Assembly Law Committee, in commenting on the FJMC candle program, noted: "The Federation of Jewish Men's Clubs is to be strongly commended for the creation of a kit for the observance of Yom HaShoah... The creation of such a ritual is an important means by which the tragedy and the lesson of the Holocaust can be transmitted to future generations. One might add that the creation of such a family and community ritual is long overdue."

From an undated FJMC brochure

SAMPLE PRESS RELEASE FOR LOCAL OR NATIONAL RELEASE

Winokur tried to find a blessing to be recited at the time of the candle lighting. His search for an appropriate blessing was brought to the attention of the Law Committee of the Rabbinical Assembly, the ruling law body of the Conservative movement, the affiliation of the Federation of Jewish Men's Clubs. Rabbi Ben Zion Bergman, the author of the Assembly's response to Winokur's request, issued an official opinion on the appropriateness of a blessing for this new activity in Jewish home observance. Rabbi Bergman suggested that, since no new blessings can be established under Jewish law, some kind of "ptichah" or meditation could be recited in the home, such as has been recited in many homes to remember the long-imprisoned Soviet dissidents, during the Passover Seder....

From a 1989 press release

MEDITATION

As I light this Yellow Candle I vow never to forget the lives of the Jewish men, women, and children who are symbolized by this flame. They were tortured and brutalized by beasts; their lives were taken in cruelty. May we be inspired to learn more about six million brothers and sisters as individuals and as communities, to recall their memory throughout the year, so that they will not suffer a double death. May we recall not only the terror of their deaths, but the splendor of so many of their lives. May the memory of their lives inspire us to hallow our own lives, and to live meaningful Jewish lives so that we may help to ensure that part of who they were shall endure always.

Written by Rabbi Jules Harlow. From the FJMC booklet "Remember The Past and Build a Better Future," 1994.

CEMENTING OF U.S. & CANADA RELATIONS

Alan Levenson (GL/U.S.) and Mort Pullan (GL/Canada) are chairing a committee to resolve the "problem" in time for the '95 campaign. Deliberations will begin in November, so that, hopefully, by next year we will have only one, unified, homogenous campaign.

From a memorandum labelled "The Yom HaShoah Yellow Yahrzeit Candle Program for 1994"

FJMC NAMES REP. TOM LANTOS HONORARY CHAIRMAN TO BEGIN 1994 YOM HASHOAH YELLOW CANDLE PROGRAM

NEW YORK, NY Feb. 3, 1994 --- Lighting a candle in every Jewish home across North America is the goal as The Federation of Jewish Men's Clubs launches its 1994 Yom HaShoah Yellow Candle™ Program. It's FJMC's most extensive program ever. The effort is being spearheaded by

U. S. Rep Tom Lantos (12th Dist., CA), the only Holocaust survivor in Congress and honorary campaign chairman....

In the New England Region, Senator Edward M. Kennedy, Nobel Laureate and honorary US Holocaust Museum chairman Elie Wiesel, U. S. Rep. Barney Frank and Bernard Cardinal Law of Boston have been named honorary regional chairpersons...

"Each generation must find new ways to contribute to the prevention of future genocides," said Lantos, who joined an anti-Nazi underground movement in his native Hungary after leaving a forced labor camp. "That's why we are encouraging Men's Clubs, Brotherhoods, Sisterhoods, and all Jewish organizations to distribute candles to families and to young people away from college. We need to keep the memory alive because Holocaust survivors are passing on and leaving us without a first person link with history."

From an FJMC press release.

NEVER AGAIN! YOM HASHOAH GUIDE

NEVER AGAIN! "To this day, there are those who insist that the Holocaust never happened – a denial of fact that is baseless and ignorant and hateful."

President Barack Obama

NEVER AGAIN! "I made the visit [to Buchenwald, April 12, 1945] deliberately, in order to be in a position to give first-hand evidence of these things if ever, in the future, there develops a tendency to charge these allegations merely to 'propaganda.'"

General Dwight D. Eisenhower

NEVER AGAIN! "When we come to the other world and meet the millions of Jews who died in the camps and they ask us, 'What have you done?' there will be many answers. You will say, 'I became a jeweler.' Another will say, 'I smuggled coffee and American cigarettes.' Another will say, 'I built houses.' But I will say, 'I didn't forget you.'"

Simon Wiesenthal

From an FJMC information packet for Yom HaShoah 5770 (2010).

THE WORLD WIDE WRAP

How do you get Jewish men to engage with a mitzvah that had been forgotten or ignored by many? The story of the World Wide Wrap is one that not only succeeded, but led to educational projects from members going into Hebrew School classrooms to teach children, to bringing in guest speakers, like a sofer (scribe), to demystify what's inside a tefillin. It would mushroom into an array of programs that include everything from "Build a Pair," where pre-b'nai mitzvah children construct model tefillin, to fundraising efforts to acquire tefillin and other ritual objects for Masorti/Conservative communities in South America and Europe.

During its 1999 Biennial convention the Federation of Jewish Men's Clubs premiered its groundbreaking film "The Ties That Bind." This film, at once both inspirational and instructive, put a new light on the experience of tefillin. Through interviews, excerpts from the Midrash and other texts, as well as a step-by-step guide to actual practice, the film offered the incentive for many men and women to adopt this mitzvah in their daily lives.

One of those so inspired was Alan Sussman, president of the Temple Israel Men's Club of Charlotte, North Carolina. In 2000 he helped come up with a program that had the simple goal of encouraging congregants to lay tefillin. His feeling was that although people did not observe the mitzvah of tefillin as often as they should or at all, this was a way to revive a tradition that for many had been lost. Alan felt that there were few ways to feel closer to God, teach the performance of a mitzvah, and get parents and children to bond in the process, than in laying tefillin: Alan has said he felt this inner vibe himself when he did it for the first time in 1992 while visiting the West Bank, where he was prompted by soldiers of the *Tzahal* (Israeli Army).

So Alan and the then vice president for publicity, Leonard Stern, thought of a response to the "Million Man March" that had happened in Washington, DC earlier that year and called it the "100 Man Wrap." It took place in May 2000 in the parking lot of Temple Israel with the full support of Rabbi Murray Ezring. As an egalitarian congregation, women were encouraged to participate as well. (Traditionally, women are exempted from time-based mitzvot such as tefillin.) In total we got 102 people to wrap collectively for the first time. Several of them had never done it before, while for many others, it was the first time they had done it since their B'nai Mitzvah. The feeling of connection was indescribable. Several of them bought their tefillin for the first time just to participate in this event, and some of those even committed to start wearing them more often.

If the goal was to reinvigorate our embracing of this mitzvah, once could not be enough. Our second World Wide Wrap happened on a Sunday in early 2001. Riding on the coattails of the success of our initial program, our second outing nearly doubled in size, with 193 people participating. It was the largest crowd our temple ever had on a day that did not coincide with a Jewish holiday. The FJMC video "The Ties that Bind" was a resounding success because it showed people who may have been felt spirituality in their hearts and minds how to actually put this into practice.

As with other ideas that came up from the clubs and spread throughout the movement by the FJMC, it evolved. Clubs held breakfast following the morning service, had video linkups to other cities joining in, educational projects like "Build a Pair" provided another way for children to participate while extending the concept to the religious schools and groups. Photos were collected from clubs around the world for the FJMC's World Wide Wrap page, with the inevitable first photos coming from congregations in Australia. As the date of the Wrap came to coincide with championship Super Bowl in February, American and Canadian participants could envy the poolside wrappers in the Southern hemisphere where it was summer.

Today the World Wide Wrap is truly global, an annual opportunity to enlist new members to engage in the mitzvah of tefillin. While this success is a source of satisfaction for the FJMC, it is also fulfilling to Alan as he scrolls through the lists of the congregations and members who enroll every year. From an idea at one club, the Wrap has been a tremendous success: helping our men's clubs grow, and maintaining one of the traditions of the Conservative/Masorti movement around the world.

Michael Abadi has served as the Masorti Olami (World Council of Synagogues) and the FJMC ambassador to Central and South America.

FROM THE RECORD

THE WORLD WIDE WRAP

A MAJOR TEFILLIN EVENT

Our club wanted to build on our previously successful annual "World Wide Wrap" by working with our USY chapter and USY region to create a major tefillin event. We coordinated the wrap with a "Build-A-Pair" program. Developed as a weekday afternoon parent/child program with our shul's Religious School (*"daled"* students - 6th grade). Flyers were sent home advertising this as a parent/child project. Dinner was provided for attendees (students and their parents). The events were a big success, with over 400 people attending the events. Most rewarding was the involvement of our youth programs.

Barry Schwartz, Temple Beth Shalom, Livingston, N.J.

TRANS-ATLANTIC TEFILLIN

As part of our yearly World Wide Wrap program, this year we held a joint trans-Atlantic program with Dor Hadash, a Masorti Kehillah in Budapest. Using Google+ Hangouts, both Temple Israel and Dor Hadash was able to transmit and project images and sound from each other. Together we learned, we *davened* and we shared *ruach*. In Sharon we had the most participants for the WWW ever.

Ron Czik, Temple Israel, Sharon, Mass.

THE TIES THAT BIND

This highly acclaimed 28-minute film is both motivational and instructional as it responds to the questions, "What will tefillin do for me?" and "Why should I wear them?" The videocassette comes in two versions - egalitarian, in which women participate, and non-egalitarian, which features only men.

From the FJMC store catalog

SPIRITUAL GUIDE

Each participant should be provided with a copy of the new spiritual guide, "First

Thoughts: A Tefillin Spiritual Primer," produced by the Federation of Jewish Men's Clubs especially for the World Wide Wrap. The guide contains the text of each of the standard blessings associated with wrapping Tefillin, but also includes numerous inspirational quotes and excerpts from text that will provide a sound spiritual basis for this mitzvah.

From the WWW Implementation Guide

FJMC TEFILLIN FUND

Our sincere thanks goes out to each of you and your clubs for planning on making the 2016 World Wide Wrap so successful. It is a great way to kick off a year of FJMC activities by generating camaraderie and mitzvah opportunities for all.

Now is a good time to take this mitzvah a step further by expanding our ability to bring new sets of tefillin to our brethren and their families in communities that need them. Please consider having your club make a World Wide Wrap 2016 donation to the FJMC Tefillin Fund.

This past year the FJMC Tefillin Fund was able to distribute sets of tefillin to clubs with special projects to use them in enhancement of their WWW plans. Additionally, we were able to distribute dozens of sets to our Masorti affiliates in Central and South America, Europe, Africa and Israel.

Irwin Harris, World Wide Wrap chairman, 2016

TEFILLIN FREQUENTLY ASKED QUESTIONS

My child is going to become a Bar/Bat Mitzvah in a few weeks. What size and type should I purchase for him/her?

It depends on your child and your community. If your child studies at a day school or if you often daven in an Orthodox environment, then we recommend the flat finish, which is most common in traditional communities. As for size, we recommend that parents order what is most suitable for their children. If your child is a regular shul-goer, you might want to consider the deluxe tefillin. However, if there is a chance the tefillin will fall in the lake at summer camp, then buy a less expensive pair.

KERUV: OPENING THE DOORS
OF THE SYNAGOGUE

Addressing issues about the reality and accelerating growth of interfaith marriage was not something the Conservative movement was eager to do. The traditional answer was to favor "in-marriage" – encouraging Jews to seek Jewish marriage partners – and to make it clear that those who married "out" would not be welcome. Conservative rabbis not only were forbidden to officiate over the marriage between a Jew and a non-Jew. Officially, they could not even attend the ceremony as a guest at risk of being kicked out of the Rabbinical Assembly.

By the 1990s it was clear that this policy was not only not preventing such marriages, but that it was leading to a steady exodus from Conservative synagogues. Few families were untouched by the growing trend, yet movement leaders had no response except to double down on responses that were now not only seen as ineffective but increasingly irrelevant. By 1997 it was clear that some new approach had to be taken, and it was the FJMC's Keruv initiative that boldly strode into the thicket where others feared to tread.

It was an extended attempt to understand and then address the accelerating realities of our present situation and its impact on the Jewish American community and the Conservative movement, its synagogue structures, its rabbis and its congregational adherent. Keruv, which means to draw near or approach, signaled a new way of dealing with families where one spouse was not Jewish but the family agreed to make a Jewish home and to raise their children as Jewish.

It was proposed that synagogues as institutions needed to reach out to interfaith couples and families and openly say, "We welcome you as you are," and not, "We welcome you, but..." It was not a matter of ignoring Halacha (Jewish law). Children of Jewish fathers and non-Jewish mothers would need to convert. The difference was that the family would not be treated as pariahs or non-beings, but as members of the community with the non-Jewish spouse included as much as allowed. Proponents argued that as young adults, our children will not go where they are not welcomed. Instead, they will make all the worst, and in all too many cases correct, assumptions about the lack of enthusiasm in welcoming interfaith couples and their children by the Conservative movement and its institutions.

Through "think tanks" and a growing number of "Keruv consultants," FJMC changed the conversation synagogue by synagogue. The goal was ensuring that Jewish families would find a home in the Conservative community, respecting the non-Jewish parent who made the commitment to raising a Jewish family. Some eventually converted and that was because they found a warm welcome instead of a cold shoulder.

It is by understanding what constitutes the structural changes necessary to be both welcoming and pro-active in that welcoming, that the FJMC Keruv Initiative believes has the capacity to grow the Conservative movement instead of chasing away our children and grandchildren. Websites were changed. Instead of being inward and circumscribed they became something truly dynamic and outward-facing, welcoming all family members committed to making a Jewish home.

In addition to many meetings with rabbis and other leaders, there was also sensitivity training for teachers and administrative staff on the issues of what it means to be an interfaith family in a Conservative synagogue, sensitivity to the realities and needs of the children of interfaith families, and sensitivity to the prejudices and tribal instincts we all carry and, in some cases, are taught. Other changes, just as important, were more subtle, as in revision of synagogue by-laws, changing what it means to be a member, in whole or part, of the Conservative Jewish community. These things are not always measurable in the neat way we might like them to be. However, there are now synagogue websites that say with clarity on their home page, "**We Welcome Interfaith Families.**"

Hannah Arendt used to say that the opposite of hate is not love, it is indifference. In the case of interfaith families, it was institutional indifference. With the Keruv Initiative the FJMC prodded the Conservative movement into replacing indifference with engagement, promoting the raising of Jewish families in ways that accommodated non-Jewish but supportive families members instead of shunning them which keeping the Jewish parent and their children within the fold.

Harvey Braunstein was co-founder of the Keruv Initiative. (This essay is an adaptation by the editor of this volume of a presentation by Braunstein on Keruv.)

FROM THE RECORD

KERUV: OPENING THE DOORS OF THE SYNAGOGUE

A BEACON OF CONSERVATIVE JUDAISM

Our initial activities were modest and our goals simple: bring the issue of interfaith families in our midst, look at the demographics and put the issue on the conservative Jewish agenda. Over more than a decade we certainly did much more than that.

In the subsequent years, endless meetings, countless telephone conversations, time spent at Pearlstone with the guys and later the gals, consultant trainings, rabbinical think tanks, and the like, have literally altered my life. Keruv has also altered the life of my synagogue, helping change it from a large, forbidding, dark, unwelcoming place to a beacon of Conservative Judaism. Where I once had to press hard just to put a link on our webpage indicating that we welcome interfaith families, something many synagogues are only getting around to, we now offer a broad range of inclusive, engaging activities, in many cases prompted and run by our supportive non-Jewish spouses and partners.

Steve Lachter, Adas Israel, Washington, DC

CLOSING THE DOORS IS NOT THE ANSWER

My first attempt fifteen years ago to find a shul for my young wife and I was disheartening. Just after we got married, we tried the local Conservative synagogue in Forest Hills, Queens, N.Y., where the rabbi made it explicitly clear, both in his words from the pulpit, and to us directly, that we were not welcome in his community. Our next try was to a Reform synagogue. While it was a nice community, a tallit, kippah, and traditional aliyot were essential parts of the Shabbat morning service to me that I realized I was not ready to give up.

From my personal experience, I quickly found my Jewish cause, to help interfaith families feel welcomed in the Conservative movement. I became deeply involved in the FJMC's Keruv initiative. Over the past decade, I have helped two shuls directly, and dozens more indirectly open their doors to interfaith families. Now living outside of Philadelphia, I can say that over the past six years, membership among our interfaith families has risen materially, as has our community support, led by our rabbi.

As I get older, raising Jewish children with lots of questions about everything, I recognize more and more that I do not know all of the answers. I do not know for sure if increased outreach efforts will stem the decline of Conservative Judaism, or Judaism in general. But what I do know for sure is that those that are arrogant enough to think that closing our doors is the answer, are certainly wrong.

Joshua Kohn, Philadelphia, Pennsylvania

NOT ON BOARD

In 2005, I was burned out running my Men's Club and just wanted to hand it over for someone else to take the reins of leadership. I was called constantly by members of the FJMC to attend convention as the FJMC's newest club. No one in my club would attend so off I went to Florida. At convention, I heard the word Keruv for the first time and attended workshops where I learned the importance of welcoming intermarried couples and their families. As it happened our shul had just done a survey to determine the breadth and needs of interfaith families in our congregation.

One committee member took it upon herself to write a letter to these couples telling them that the rules of United Synagogue would not allow a non-Jewish member to vote. A few of these couples said they were going to quit because they had begun to feel they were unwelcome. When I told Rabbi Simon about this he told me that as soon as convention was over he would call our rabbi and advise him on how to handle this situation. The day after convention he kept his word and called our rabbi and talked to him for an hour and a half.

When I returned to talk to our rabbi about convention I told him about Keruv and he was not on board. A few months later at work I received a call from Rabbi Simon telling me that he wanted to train me as a Keruv Consultant.

Phil Snyder, Tifereth Israel, San Diego, California

KNOWLEDGE IS A KEY ELEMENT OF KERUV

It's been about seventeen years since my first Keruv Consultant training opportunity in Los Angeles. As a convert to Judaism, I am very much concerned with interfaith outreach by our community. At that first training meeting, I was one of a group of men from different areas of the country, all of us sharing a general concept of the need for better interfaith relations in response to rising rates of interfaith marriage. Keruv outreach focuses attention on respectful discourse with others.

One of our issues in this endeavor is our own lack of understanding of Judaism and how we portray Judaism to the Jewish and non-Jewish community. Often, I have encountered Jews who have only a rudimentary knowledge of their own religion. Such a lack of knowledge makes for a difficult discussion of religious differences with our loved-ones.

And so I have come to view knowledge as a key element of Keruv. Knowledge of our own beliefs and knowledge of how to express those beliefs in a respectful manner makes for a successful interfaith encounter.

Bob Carroll, Shomrei Torah, West Hills, California

SHARING OUR STORY

I was first drafted into the Keruv Initiative by my rabbi of blessed memory, Steven Tucker, who had just returned from one of Rabbi Simon's early Rabbinic Think-Tanks in 2004. I was, he said, the ideal candidate as I had lived the life of the Supportive Non-Jewish Spouse in our Temple community for a number of years. With the help of a couple of Keruv-trained mentors, Bob Carroll and Ken Elfand, we quickly planned an introductory six-session program (modeled after FJMC's Hearing Men's Voices program) called "Let's Talk About It."

Those sessions changed lives. It changed the lives of those who attended and participated. It changed the culture of our synagogue. And it changed me.

One change, which took years to recognize, was that I had not been truly welcomed when we joined our Temple; I was tolerated. I was not included in conversations after services. I was not invited to engage in deeper learning by other members – I was allowed to be present, and only the rabbi truly helped me to move along my Jewish journey that led to my choice to become Jewish after 17 years of marriage.

After getting started in Keruv, I attended the next training weekend. During that training, we were supposed to hear from a few couples at a nearby synagogue about their experiences as inter-married families in their synagogue community. One of the training organizers had asked for my wife, Linda, and I to be available as a back-up if one or more of these couples did not show. As it turned out, we were the only ones there to speak and we told our story. By the time we finished talking, looking mostly at each other, we noticed to our amazement that the entire group had tears in their eyes.

The impact that sharing our story had on the group helped us realize that women needed to be a part of the Keruv initiative if it was going to be truly successful. What was initially a Men's Club initiative has since evolved into a truly egalitarian effort.

Alex Romano, Temple Aliyah, Northridge, California

HEARTS AND MINDS

I remember being at an FJMC executive board meeting in 2001 Convention in Toronto, when the then taboo topic of interfaith marriage was initially discussed. Many of us began to openly share how we had been personally impacted by the institutional and cultural obstacles that hindered our ability to integrate interfaith families into our communities. The thought of being unable to keep our children and grandchildren in our synagogue communities had become unbearable.

Immediately following, Rabbi Simon and our leadership convened a think tank in New York's Catskills to examine this challenge. I recall sitting around the table contemplating how we, the men of the FJMC, could take on the almost inconceivable task of changing the attitudes, reactions and responses of the Conservative Movement – its institutions, rabbis and lay leaders – when faced with an multi-faith couple pre- or post-marriage before the non-Jewish partner chooses to convert. I was never more proud to be a member of FJMC – to participate in a conversation which, in time, would lead to an initiative that caused a dynamic shift in the thinking of the Conservative movement.

It continues to be far more than what we envisioned that afternoon in Toronto. Hearts and minds have been changed forever. FJMC has been and, certainly with regard to Keruv, needs to continue to be, the point of the arrow.

Norm Kurtz, Beth Judea, Buffalo Grove, Illinois

HOUSEHOLD MEMBERSHIPS

During the ten years that I spent serving as a Keruv Consultant, our annual gatherings produced some remarkable programs and initiatives. Not the least of which was the language crafted to create a synagogue membership category for interfaith couples. The name of the category was to be called "Household Memberships". It was an early effort to have the synagogue itself be a reflection of the welcoming spirit of its membership.

Having served on my synagogue board for more years than I wish to count, I was prepared to introduce the Household Membership category to my fellow officers and board members. In keeping with good politics, I sought out the approval of our newly installed president. Four years and two presidents went by without any effort being given to the adoption of the membership category. It became clear to me that I was going to have to assume the office of president, which I did in 2009.

The officers and board went through the procedures to add this membership category to our by-laws. At the end of my first year as president, a motion to adopt the category went before the synagogue membership at the annual meeting. The dialogue was so contentious by just a few people, that a motion was made and passed to table the adoption until the next annual election.

In 2010, I invited Rabbi Chuck Simon to serve as a weekend Scholar In-Residence. For two days Chuck brilliantly addressed my congregation as to the importance of interfaith welcoming. At the time of the annual election, the Household Membership category was overwhelmingly adopted by our membership. It would not have been possible to succeed in this accomplishment without the support and participation of Rabbi Simon.

Al Simon, Mequon, Wisconsin

I HAVE COME A LONG WAY

Out of the blue I got a phone call from Rabbi Simon, personally inviting me to attend a Keruv seminar in Florida. As I was at a small synagogue in New Jersey, the chance to go to warmer climes seemed just the thing. I wasn't particularly familiar with the new Keruv initiative. As for my position on outreach to non-Jews, let's just say that I was very much a product of the movement as it was back in those days: I was publicly and proudly outspoken about the need to "circle the wagons" and protect ourselves against the scourge of intermarriage. I was still, in those days, buying into what I now call "anxiety-based Judaism" – one that places fear of non-Jewish grandchildren higher than meaningful and transformative Jewish experiences for those who are alive right now.

When I arrived I was thrilled to join with other rabbis and lay leaders at that conference who were willing to ask previously taboo questions in our movement. Prior to Chuck, I just didn't imagine such openness possible within our halachically and boundaried community. Yes, indeed. I have come a long way since then.

Inspired by his example, I pioneered first a special "Keruv Aliyah" in my congregation in Washington DC, and then moved on to full-blown aufrufs for all couples getting married, whether or not it is an intermarriage. I have come to see that we must look beyond the smaller thinking of earlier generations, and be willing to be proud and confident, courageous and joyful about the authentic brand of Judaism that our movement offers. I have learned that the more loving and welcoming we are, the more committed and vibrant all our families are. I have learned that when we not only "tolerate" non-Jews, not only "welcome" non-Jews, but genuinely integrate non-Jews and challenge them to weave their lives and their authentic paths into the fabric of our Jewish communities, the holiness and vibrancy of the whole community is only enhanced.

Rabbi Gil Steinlauf, Adas Israel, Washington, DC

CHALLENGING MY ATTITUDES

I received a phone call from Rabbi Chuck Simon with an invitation to participate in a gathering of rabbis that was being convened to explore the question of intermarried families within synagogue life. At that time, there were few efforts to welcome intermarried families into synagogue life and certainly nothing within the Conservative movement. I can't remember whether it was billed as a "conference" or a "seminar", but I do remember my reluctance to attend. I already considered myself quite advanced in this area and didn't honestly think there was much I could learn from Men's Club. But then I received a follow up call from Chuck and soon learned that it was impossible to say "no" to him. God knows I tried, but he just wouldn't take no for an answer. That was how I first encountered Chuck and got my first exposure to his relentless, no-nonsense, approach to challenging the status quo.

It was at that first gathering of rabbis that I began to challenge my own attitudes towards the acceptance of non-Jews in synagogue. Chuck forced me to ask the questions, "Do I need to exclude the non-Jew from this activity?" and "Am I really conveying a feeling of welcome to non-Jews?" Whether it was life cycle experiences or synagogue programs when I began to challenge assumptions of involvement by non-Jewish spouses and parents as committed members of the community, I could see their experience differently. As I began to reflect on my attitudes and the policies of the synagogue, I began to realize that I was not as embracing of intermarrieds as I thought. It was a result of that first experience that transformed my entire approach towards intermarried families

Rabbi Stewart L. Vogel, Temple Aliyah, Woodland Hills, California

FINDING A WELCOMING SPIRITUAL HOME

In the Jewish world, Jews who married "out" were considered failures or rejectionists. When the 1990 Jewish Federation census came out, panic ran through the world of American Jewish leadership. More than 50 percent of new marriages involving a Jew were to a person who was not Jewish. The "continuity" industry was born. The leading Jewish sociologists promulgated the same statistical "truths." The sociologists told us that grandchildren of intermarriage ceased to be Jewish by the second generation. American Jewry was on a direct linear path to total assimilation and decline.

In the Conservative movement, one response to the "crisis" of intermarriage was the decision to strengthen the walls of separation. There were those who argued that any act of welcoming of the intermarried would send a message of acceptable normative behavior. They argued that if rabbis would only maintain a united front against officiating, young people would not be encouraged to marry "outside" the faith. While intermarried families could become members in the congregation, the non-Jewish partner could have no role in membership, leadership, or ritual. Indeed, a Jew married to a non-Jew could not teach or have any significant role in the synagogue lest people get the impression that intermarriage was condoned.

Rabbi Chuck Simon did not see the world of love and marriage as a binary choice. Every marriage is an intermarriage in terms of joining together two individuals coming from different families of origin, values, and social patterns. He recognized that couples need to define the values and stories that will shape their own family's identity. In doing so, they could be encouraged to make Jewish choices. He knew that Judaism can add a new depth of meaning to a home that is enriched by Shabbat, the holidays, and Tikkun Olam, the Mending or Repairing of the World. If only the non-Jewish partner in an intermarriage could find a welcoming spiritual home within the Jewish community, he or she would begin to identify with Jewish culture and faith. Rather than rejecting and condemning the intermarried, Chuck sought to bring them closer within the folds of the Jewish world.

Today, many non-Jewish partners of Jewish spouses are choosing to create Jewish homes and raise Jewish children. They celebrate Jewish holidays and rituals. They become active participants in the life of the synagogue. Formal conversion to Judaism may come – or not.

If and when it does, that conversion may not happen for a number of years. And then, only after having lived, essentially, an otherwise Jewish life.

Rabbi Sam Gordon, Congregation Sukkat Shalom, Wilmette, Illinois

SPEAKING UP WHEN NO ONE ELSE WOULD

My entry into the world of Keruv was born out of necessity. I came to the Anshe Emet Synagogue in 1982. Because of the congregation's urban setting, I had the opportunity to engage with a number of young couples, and with it came requests for conversion study. At the time, there was a joint conversion class in Chicago under the auspices of the Reform Movement. After teaching one of the cohorts of the class, I found it to be inconsistent and utterly inadequate for my students. The problem was that my rabbinical school experience at JTS left me unprepared for this situation. I do not remember ever discussing conversion or intermarriage in a serious way during my years of study, in either New York or Israel.

The sad fact is that while there are a few excellent conversion programs in the United States, neither the Rabbinical Assembly nor the United Synagogue have ever taken the issue seriously. How else can one explain the lack of consistency between conversion programs from city to city, or the wide spectrum of approaches to Keruv between synagogues? In fact, the only organization of the Conservative Movement to show any real interest in developing a thoughtful approach to Keruv has been the FJMC.

While I am happy to note that other arms of the movement are now taking the issue of intermarriage and conversion more seriously, the fact remains that the FJMC focused attention on this vital issue when no one else in a position of authority would.

Rabbi Michael Siegel, Anshe Emet, Chicago, Illinois

COMBINED FAMILY AT B'NAI MITZVAH

Before my Keruv training, if an interfaith couple wanted to have a bar or bat mitzvah, the non-Jewish parent and the Jewish parent would co-present the tallit to their child together – and that was it. It turned out, we could do better! Now, when we conduct the intergenerational Torah pass, we have the Jewish family line up in generational order, from eldest to the child at the ark. Then on the other side of the child, we line up the non-Jewish family, from eldest to youngest. I pass the Torah down the Jewish line, to the child. Then I talk about the values the child received from his non-Jewish family line, and explain that all these influences made the child the mensch he or she is today. The idea was to move beyond merely "tolerating" the non-Jewish side of the family, to celebrating and welcoming it.

When we get to the parents' 7th Aliyah, the non-Jewish parent and the Jewish parent ascend the bima together. Then the non-Jewish parent sits on a chair of honor while the Jewish parent takes the Aliyah. When the Aliyah is completed, I have the Jewish and non-Jewish parent stand side-by-side, and I bless the two of them together, explaining it took both of their memberships to our shul, each taking turns schlepping their child to lessons, and their overall support, that got the child to this milestone. Then I have them stand together to witness their child's special maftir Aliyah as a Jewish adult.

Rabbi Michael Beals, Beth Shalom, Wilmington, Delaware

BUILDING SHABBAT COMMUNITY

Why is it that when the subject of attending Shabbat morning services comes up in conversation, many people just change the subject or sometimes answer flat out that that part of Jewish life is not for them? One can come up with numerous reasons, and if you've tried to encourage people to come to services, no doubt you've heard them: other activities have a higher priority than sitting in shul for three hours; other practices are more "spiritual"; and, perhaps more often than we would like, they do not find the Shabbat prayer experience itself as being especially meaningful. Even for people who attend regularly, some of these feelings may arise.

When people attend services, they seem to enter the synagogue without any clear expectations of what they expect to gain from the experience. Think about it. What are our "goals" when we attend Shabbat morning services? Do we possess sufficient skills and knowledge to make prayer service attendance meaningful and worthwhile?

What about our rabbis and cantors and other leaders? As "providers" of these services, do our clergy and lay leaders consider what we should envision as an outcome for those who choose to attend? Will congregants be moved? Challenged? Educated? Inspired? Motivated? Comforted? Will being part of a Shabbat community enrich their lives? What is the point of being there?

The FJMC recognized that, as individuals, we can each have a different experience and a different outcome. Given that, it focused on the variety of goals of attendees, creating a program to address the challenge of poor attendance on Shabbat morning in our synagogues. The Building Shabbat Community initiative was premised upon the idea that we can successfully inspire more people to attend Shabbat morning services if we take the time to develop and offer a choice of meaningful prayer and study experiences.

We began with the sad but true fact that the vast majority of North American Masorti/Conservative synagogues fail to attract a significant percentage of their community to Shabbat morning services. According to recent data, less than five percent of affiliated Conservative synagogue members attend Shabbat morning services regularly (at least once a month). It seems obvious that if an individual doesn't attend services the likelihood that they will have a personally meaningful Shabbat experience will be less.

In order to rectify this situation, vibrant and interesting alternatives were needed to encourage our members to become engaged with the beauty of Shabbat. If Shabbat was seen as a burden instead of a blessing, something important was being lost.

In 2015 the FJMC published <u>Building Shabbat Community</u>, authored by FJMC past International Presidents Robert Braitman and Norm Kurtz. It contained a discussion and implementation guide of suggested alternative approaches to the Shabbat Morning Prayer experience. This manual was designed for those who are interested in enhancing the experience of *tefilah* (prayer) in their communities, whatever their level of experience.

One of the innovations was the "Learner's Service" which recognized that, for many, the service was a performance being staged for them rather than something in which they should and could actively participate. This program was developed as a six week experience running parallel to the congregation's main Shabbat morning service. The concept is to teach by exploring each prayer in the service to include the *p'shat* (the literal meaning) of what the prayer says as well as to include a *drash* (an interpretation) providing deeper meaning, insight and inspiration for each aspect of the service. The program is intended to inspire learning, participation, and growth for potential prayer leaders in the community by demystifying the service. Congregants who understand what they're doing and why, and come to appreciate the structure of the service, become more engaged.

Another innovation was the "Interpretive/Experiential Service," which was designed as a service for adults, regardless of whether they were literate in Hebrew, who wished to share community on Shabbat morning. Those who attended found an inviting opportunity to participate in a regular Shabbat Morning Prayer experience and Torah discussion as well as the chance to improve their understanding of Shabbat, of prayer and of Torah. This welcoming inclusive service was designed to be offered as an ongoing weekly alternative running parallel to the "traditional" service. Each week, attendees would be encouraged to attend this service or the traditional service as they chose. As people grew comfortable and familiar with the service they might attend the "traditional" service which was less opaque for them; likewise some Shabbat "regulars" appreciated having the opportunity to engage in a more relaxed format.

In the right environment – with the positive support of clergy and lay leaders – an alternative prayer experience can help to create a warm and welcoming prayer community; develop a service which conforms to the rituals and traditions of Conservative Judaism; present a service which is accessible and non-threatening regardless of level of Hebrew language fluency or of prayer familiarity; assure that the opportunity to learn and to develop prayer skills and Torah knowledge occurs each Shabbat morning for adults of all ages and backgrounds; and provide a parallel experience which supplements the established minyan. There is also the opportunity to integrate the two services for the concluding prayers and for the community Kiddush.

In the tradition of the FJMC, this initiative wasn't simply presented to the world. It is the result of numerous field tests of these programs, including the FJMC's implementation guide and comprehensive training at FJMC conventions and retreats. These two programs, as well as other variations of alternative parallel Shabbat morning services, are now being successfully implemented in numerous Masorti/Conservative communities across North America. Clergy and lay leadership who have agreed to experiment with the introduction of alternative service experiences have universally recognized their successes. With pride, the FJMC notes that as a direct result of its "Building Shabbat Community" initiative, many congregants who did not attend Shabbat morning services in the past are now joining the minyan, and are experiencing a joyful and meaningful Shabbat experience of their own.

Norm Kurtz is a past international president of the FJMC.

FROM THE RECORD
BUILDING SHABBAT COMMUNITY

MAKE IT YOUR OWN

These materials are just a beginning. There are several excellent publications available to you to enhance your Shabbat programming. We have provided a variety of those references at the end of the manual. Remember that it is important to tailor your teachings to the demographic of those who are attending your service. Comments that are meaningful to one group may not resonate in the same way with another.

Bob and Norm present two "models" that have a proven track record as well as practical advice on how to get started. Feel free to use these models or adapt them to what works best in your own community. You will notice that there is considerable overlap between these models. Again, take what is most applicable to your setting and make it your own.

From the Making Shabbat Community implementation guide.

THE LEARNER'S MINYAN

Knowledge: give attendees the basic information that they need to understand what happens during the service and to comprehend the meaning of the prayers

Meaning: Provide a context for the prayer experience that resonates with their lives. Why is this experience meaningful to them? To view prayer from a variety of perspectives – God as Creator, God as Revealer, and God as a personal and caring "partner." Can religious language be beneficial even when faith and belief is in doubt?

From the Making Shabbat Community implementation guide.

WELCOME SHABBAT

Saturday morning Shabbat minyan services at TBI are always warm, welcoming and inclusive but once a month we go the extra mile to welcome our upcoming b'nei mitzvah students, newcomers of all ages and anyone who would like a little bit more explanation about the why's and how's of our Saturday morning services.

* Torah School teacher, Joseph Tepperman explains it all for us.

* Please don't be shy. We guarantee that even old-timers are bound to learn something new.

* Students will be welcome up on the bima to see what all the mystery is about.

* Check our calendar page for the next Shabbat Welcome Minyan (usually the 4th Saturday of each month).

* See you soon!

From Temple Beth Israel, Los Angeles, California.

THE WELLNESS CHALLENGE

On a warm Chicago evening in 2007, I stood before the attendees at the FJMC Biennial Convention for the final time as the organization's president to offer a "farewell address." The speech was what one would expect, a summary of recent accomplishments as well as setting out some goals for the upcoming years. As I looked around the room however, I was moved to say the following:

> It is traditional for an outgoing president to leave an inspirational word or a challenge for the future. So, my friends and this is from the heart.

> Guys, I'm worried about your health. There are simply too many overweight men here at the convention and in our men's clubs. In the spirit of this Shabbat Mattot, I want each of you to take a vow. Vow to see your doctor and lose the weight by the time of the next convention. I'm issuing a challenge tonight:

> 1. To our clubs, to devise programming to help you achieve this goal
> 2. To the incoming leadership team, to make this issue a priority
> 3. And to each of you, to make and keep this vow.

Ten years have elapsed since that Chicago evening. Frankly, much of my "farewell address" has been long forgotten but my challenge for FJMC to become a leader in the promoting the health of the men in our ranks resonates to this day.

On an individual basis, numerous men have contacted me with the news of their success in losing weight, by starting an exercise regime and so on. What is even more exciting however is how our Men's Clubs and FJMC as an organization have stepped up in numerous ways to be advocates for men's health.

Shortly after the Chicago convention, a Men's Health Committee was formed. The committee produced a monthly publication, "Wellness News," with ideas for club programming and inspiration for individual involvement. A challenge was issued across the organization to "Walk to the Convention."

During the two years leading up to the convention in 2009, Men's Clubs were asked to recruit members who would commit to an exercise regime. Records were kept of those activities and various "miles" accorded on the goal of "walking" to the convention. Nearly two dozen clubs participated with well over 100 men enrolled.

Men's Health has continued to be a major initiative of FJMC. Indeed, a criterion for a club to earn a "Quality Club Award" is having a health and wellness program in place. In addition, the organization's Torch Award competition includes a category for programming related to Men's Health. Clubs have had informational programs about diet and exercise, have initiated bike trips, facilitated gym memberships and so much more.

The latest salvo in this campaign is the regular publication of a Health and Wealth Newsletter. Each issue has important information highlighting the numerous ways that men can enhance their well-being. As we look to the future, FJMC stands at the forefront of advocacy for men's health in the Jewish community.

Robert E. Braitman, M.D. is a past international president of the FJMC.

FROM THE RECORD

THE WELLNESS CHALLENGE

BODY AND SPIRIT

Body and Spirit: Men Staying Healthy and Fit represents the second major publication in the "Hearing Men's Voices" series... We place a premium on our health and the good life derived from being healthy. The aim of a healthy lifestyle is to prevent and/or delay the development of a disease. Certain steps are necessary beyond simply "lifestyle" to make this happen. This involves visits to the physician for health screening and preventive medical measures, as well as timely visits when symptoms occur.

From Body and Spirit (1999)

PLUMBING PROBLEMS

Men's health concerns have been gaining increasing attention during the past decade. This may in part be a response to the focus on specific women's concerns during the 1970s and 1980s, as well as a rise in self-awareness and a sense of vulnerability on the part of men....

Men's health is certainly not limited to the areas mention in this article. Certainly many more problems relate equally to men and women. But the problems addressed here [prostate disease, erectile dysfunction] are specific to middle-aged and elderly men. They are significant and can be life-threatening when ignored. No longer should there be embarrassed silence with respect to what were once taboo subjects.

Dr. Michael Ziegelbaum, in Body and Spirit

A JEWISH PERSPECTIVE ON HEALTH AND WELLNESS

From your mother's chicken soup or "Jewish Penicillin" to the admonition in Genesis to eat the fruits and vegetables of the trees and shrubs, our tradition emphasizes taking care of yourself. In the book of Exodus, we are instructed to cut the fat away from meat, advice offered thousands of years before we ever heard it from Jean Mayer, dean of the School of Public Health at Harvard University in the 1960s.

We all live with an illusion of immortality. But, taking care of yourself is simply not an option any longer. Today, many men are getting the health message as businesses put a greater value on keeping their employees and managers healthy. Many of us are involved in our jobs, our families, our synagogues and men's clubs and only pay attention to health after we get sick. It may not be too late then for some illnesses, but by doing that we run the risk of missing the opportunity to maintain our health.

I am going to ask you to both consider the status of your health and improve your habits of daily living. No one can take better care of you than you do, but simply waiting to get sick and see a doctor just won't do. Waiting until after you are sick is like calling the plumber after your basement is flooded. The damage is already done.

David Heber, M.D., from Jewish Men at the Crossroads (2013).

WHY DON'T MEN SEEK HEALTH CARE?

Men also don't like to be told what to do. Whether we call it controlling behavior or fear of admitting being wrong, this factor may also account for much of the reluctance men have to seek medical attention. Predictable reprimands to watch the diet, cut down on alcohol, stop smoking, lose weight, reduce stress, or exercise more frequently can be a disincentive to entering a provider's office. The doctor may be categorized as a critical authority figure in a man's life, rather than an ally to promote wellbeing. Maybe for this reason, fifty-eight percent of men say that something prevents them from going to a doctor for routine care. Everything from a lack of health insurance to preferring natural treatments gets in the way. They know what their doctors will tell them, in any event, so why subject themselves to the cost, time, hassle, and process of humiliation?

Paul Davidson, Ph. D., from Jewish Men at the Crossroads.

A MATCH MADE IN HEAVEN: THE RAMAH/FJMC PARTNERSHIP

One of the priorities for the FJMC was getting clubs to see beyond the walls of their own synagogues. One of the ways of promoting this ideas was to strengthen regional identity so that members felt a feeling of brotherhood towards other men's clubs in the region, participating in retreats, awards dinners, and other regional activities. The involvement with the Ramah camps was truly special in that it benefitted both groups, and was unique in that no other arm of the movement committed itself to supporting Ramah the way the FJMC did.

I am reminded of Theodor Herzl's immortal words, "If you will it, it is no dream; and if you do not will it, a dream it is and a dream it will stay." Herzl's words couldn't be truer as I recall the dream of Lee Linder (of Blessed Memory), a past International Vice President of FJMC.

Lee knew how important Jewish education is for our children, and saw an especially successful program at Camp Ramah in the Poconos. So he gathered a group of dedicated men from the FJMC's Middle Atlantic Region and, under the presidency of Stephen Davidoff, began to run concerts. Started in 1982, "The Golden Kippah Youth Concerts" have raised one million dollars, allowing Camp Ramah in the Poconos to build an Indoor Activities Center, and complete a half-million dollar renovation of the children's bunks.

Their commitment didn't end there. According to Davidoff, the Middle Atlantic Region launched a multi-million dollar Scholarship Endowment so that children who want to go to Ramah can go. In addition, the "Tour de Shul" Bike Ride dedication towards Ramah, which was originated by the New England Region and has spread elsewhere, remains very strong in the Middle Atlantic Region, according to Past President Larry Allen.

FJMC has encouraged regions to support their local Ramah camps, figuring the benefit flows in two directions. Ramah gets another source of support, while FJMC members not only bond with another part of the Conservative movement, but may find the fathers of campers taking a new interest in the clubs at their own shuls as they learn of FJMC's commitment to Ramah.

Although individual synagogues sometimes offered scholarships to the children of member families, this direct support to the camp brought the involvement to a whole new level. It is believed that the origin for the idea came from the Western Region which supported Camp Ramah in Ojai, California with their successful fundraising programs called the "Red Yarmulke" dinners (named for the signature red kippahs of the region). According to regional past President Bart Kogan, the dinners began in 1977.

Some of the fundraising was for general purposes, or for construction of new facilities, as when the Great Lakes Region raised money for a guest facility for Camp Ramah in Canada. Others were more specifically targeted. A new program was introduced to Bart called the TIKVAH program, which focused on allowing children with special needs to share in the Ramah camping experience. Seed money was needed to launch this at Camp Ramah in Ojai.

Once again, FJMC came through. They committed half the proceeds from the next Red Yarmulke dinner to TIKVAH, and with the help of a very generous contribution from the caterer Murray Cohen, they were off and running.

As the relationship between the Ramah Camps and FJMC continued, another new program was developing at Camp Ramah in the Berkshires. According to Shelly Handel it was to be Breira B'Ramah, an overnight Jewish camping experience for children with social and learning challenges. FJMC did significant fundraising and helped Camp Ramah launch the very successful Breira program which has helped hundreds of children over the past 15 years.

In almost every region in the country, FJMC has helped and supported Ramah in many ways, coming with new fundraising programs, upgrading facilities, and (see below) even helping to launch a new Ramah from the ground up.

The children at all of the Ramah camps have benefited greatly from generous dedication of the leadership of the FJMCs which will have a lasting impact for years to come on the Conservative movement.

Richard Skolnik is Past Chair, Camp Ramah, Berkshires, and Immediate Past President, USCJ.

FROM THE RECORD

A MATCH MADE IN HEAVEN:
THE RAMAH/FJMC PARTNERSHIP

NEW ENGLAND GOES TO CAMP

Since 1970, Camp Ramah in New England has offered a special program to meet the social and religious needs of developmentally challenged Jewish adolescents. The Tikvah ("hope") Program provides the full Ramah experience – swimming, boating, sports, the arts, dance, dramatics, and more – under the supervision of specially trained staff. Like all Ramah campers, Tikvah campers receive intensive Jewish education that includes Judaic classes, daily religious services, Hebrew language, and bar and bat mitzvah training.

The New England Region of FJMC has been sponsoring events in support of the Tikvah Program at Camp Ramah, located in Palmer, Massachusetts, since the early 1990s. The events have included a raffle, a concert and most recently, the region's Tour de Shuls. Several Tikvah leaders and Tikvah campers participate as riders and/or helpers in the annual event.

Since the relationship began, the region has given the camp over $100,000. In addition to a hand-scribed scroll of Lamentations donated to the camp, region leaders personally purchased three sailboats which are named for FJMC activities: World Wide Wrap, Yellow Candle and Art of Jewish Living.

In 2001, the region relocated its annual retreat to Camp Ramah in New England. The retreat, formerly named the Laymen's Institute, celebrated its 71st year in June 2017. The retreat, held every year since its inception in 1945, is the oldest continuous Jewish men's retreat in the United States.

In recognition of the region's strong and ongoing commitment to Camp Ramah in New England, the camp has placed a permanent plaque of appreciation in honor of the region's support of Ramah and its Tikvah Program.

Arnie Miller, New England Region past president

A CAMP IS BORN

Some 25 years ago, after moving to Nashville, I approached our shul's president, wanting to start a men's club. My wonderful childhood memories of going to father and son men's club breakfasts spurred me to feel the need to develop a brotherhood in my new shul. I knew little of the FJMC, so I called Rabbi Simon who was very excited to have a new, affiliated club in the southeast. He suggested using the Yom HaShoah candle program to kick start our club. We were very successful not only financially, but with the tremendous reception we received by the West End Synagogue.

Rabbi Chuck invited me to attend the international convention at the Split Rock Resort in the Poconos the summer of '93. He was not only a most gracious host to Ruthi and I, but he introduced us to a group of men from other southeast communities, including Alan Sussman, from Charlotte. Wisely gauging mine and Alan's tremendous excitement about convention, he asked us to spearhead the creation of a new Southeast Region of FJMC, later named Anshei Darom. Thus began a 24-year quest, a virtual labor of love, which started with Anshei Darom and soon thereafter included the establishment in 1997 of Ramah Darom, the first southern Ramah camp and Jewish Retreat Center.

Without his wisdom, insight and support, I don't think Alan and I would have embarked upon our journey. We suggested to Chuck that, given the geographic spread of a Southeast region (Memphis in west Tennessee to Mobile in southern Alabama), we would need some type of meaningful project to bring such a region together. Chuck smiled, with that all-knowing grin that said, "Do I have the right guy for you guys to meet."

Chuck introduced us to Rabbi Shelly Dorf, then head of the National Ramah Commission. The NRC had tried, unsuccessfully in the 60's, to start a southern Ramah camp. Would we be interested in working on such a project? Well, what happens when two "can do" kind of guys are presented with the opportunity of a lifetime? With Chuck's encouragement, Alan and I became passionately involved in bringing together key players within the Conservative movement. At a meeting in Charlotte just four months later, and with Chuck having obtained a pledge of $40,000 from three FJMC members who were former Ramah campers themselves, the idea of Ramah

Darom was born. The $40k was matched at that meeting, a feasibility study arranged and a founding board was created.

Now, 24 years since that '93 convention at Split Rock, Ramah Darom has established itself as one of the premier Jewish institutions in the South, if not in the nation. It is a magical place where thousands of young Jewish children have experienced life changing growth and development and where adults have communed for intense, extraordinary retreat programs.

Gene Sacks, West End Synagogue, Brentwood, Tennessee

HEARING MEN'S VOICES: A CASE STUDY

The "Hearing Men's Voices" initiative has been one of the most popular and successful items on FJMC's agenda. These three essays map out the process that could be applied to the other initiatives in this book: going from club to international organization and back to the clubs, where it continues to evolve.

IN THE BEGINNING

In 1997 I spoke at the FJMC International Convention in the Catskills at the Concord resort. It was the second time that I addressed one of our conventions about what would become our "Hearing Men's Voices" initiative.

After I checked in and got my badge, I proceeded to go up to my room to settle in. As I stood alone in the elevator, weary from the drive up from Philadelphia, I was grateful for some solitary time. But just as the doors were closing a woman (who was not with our convention) stuck her hand between them and they popped open. She stepped onto the elevator. Disappointed that I was no longer alone with my thoughts, I tried to give a smile that was enough to be polite but not so welcoming as to invite conversation. But she was not deterred.

"What are you speaking about?" she asked. I was nonplussed. How did she know I was speaking? "Your name tag. It says you are a speaker. What are you speaking about?"

Eager to keep the conversation to a minimum, I answered somewhat curtly, "Men's issues."

I'll never forget her reply. "Harumph," she said. "What issues do men have?!"

I must say that a few years earlier I probably would have said the same thing. I was ordained by JTS in 1972, and my early years in the rabbinate were dominated by the movement to achieve equal rights for women in Judaism. My first Rabbinical Assembly convention was notable for the presence of a group called *"Ezrat Nashim."* Denied by the hierarchy of a slot on the official program, this group of a dozen young women came to the RA convention to make their case for equal rights. Women should count in the minyan, they argued. They should be able to read Torah. They should be able to be rabbis and *hazzanim.* It seems quaint today. But their agenda was revolutionary at the time and it would dominate the Jewish world during that period. It was both a result of the feminist awakening in the larger society, and the growing consciousness of Jewish women who had been educated just like men, but were denied prominent communal participatory and leadership roles.

While I had given a lot of thought to women's issues, I never realized that that the changing role of women had led to a changing consciousness among men as well. Men's voices were often silent, hesitant to speak out for fear of being labeled anti-feminist. Into this vacuum, the FJMC developed "Hearing Men's Voices." I was proud to be part of the initial stages of this initiative.

I first became aware of "men's issues" when, by chance, I read an article in the *Philadelphia Inquirer* in 1990 on Father's Day. It was about a men's retreat led by a Harvard psychologist, Dr. Samuel Osherson. The focus of the retreat was on the often conflicted role of men and their fathers. But that was only the portal for exploring the emotional life of men in our society, and how, in the wake of the feminist movement, it was changing in ways that challenged a man's sense of self.

The classic male role in society was one of the strong provider, the defender of the family, the rock everyone could lean on in times of emotional, physical and economic turmoil. Men were supposed to subdue their emotions, never entertaining doubt or fear, in order to fulfil their male role with unflagging resolve. Society depended on it. Our families depended on it.

The feminist movement, however, challenged, perhaps unwittingly, the classic male stereotype. Women were increasingly pursuing their own careers. They could not be the only nurturers in the family and sought out – really, they expected – participation from their male partners. It was not enough for a father to demonstrate love by working hard and protecting the family. He had to learn to be an equal partner at home, and become a co-nurturer with his spouse. The emotional reserve that had been necessary to function effectively as a male in society did not work when it came to diapering a baby or nursing a hurt knee. And some "strong" men felt challenged when their wives' careers were more lucrative than their own. The feminist movement unveiled an emotional tier of consciousness that men did not know existed in their psyche. And they did not know what to do with it.

I related to the *Inquirer* article viscerally. As a son, and as the father of three sons, the article struck a responsive chord. In particular, it led me to focus on my memories of my father who died when I was only 24. What was he all about? What was my relationship with him? What was the unfinished business I had with him? I realized I didn't know much about him. I asked my sister. What's there to know, she said, he worked all the time! I spoke to other men in the congregation and realized they had the same reaction, and the same feelings that they wanted to know more about their fathers, and about the changing role of being a man.

In the fall of 1991, I offered a workshop "For Men Only" in an inter-congregational study program we had in our community. Some women were upset about being excluded (although by then there were plenty of women's consciousness-raising groups). But I was convinced that men needed a safe space where they could express themselves without the fear of feeling shamed in front of women.

The program was a huge success. One of the participants was Larry Allen, then international president of the FJMC. Larry was touched by the discussions, and the emotions that were being elicited. Not long after that I was invited to address the 1993 FJMC Convention at Split Rock Lodge in the Poconos.

It was a revelatory experience. The response to my talk, but even more to a workshop I gave entitled "Finding our Fathers," was thunderous. Men surprised themselves as they spoke about their relationships with their fathers. It was as if a scab had been ripped from a wound. Aged men spoke about their long dead fathers with tears in their eyes. Some fathers and sons who sat side by side wept as they hugged each other.

When I spoke to the biennial convention in 1997, there was some discussion about the FJMC doing a series of pamphlets which would contain essays on topics of "men's issues". They would focus on relating to our fathers, our livelihood, health, religion and other issues. Most of all, they would focus on how we relate to ourselves. A prototype pamphlet edited by Dr. Robert E. Braitman was distributed at the convention. It included my keynote address, "Limping Jacob's Limp," and source material which was used in six workshops at the convention on areas of change and challenge to the role of men in contemporary society. It was distributed to all the clubs after the convention with the expressed hope that it would be "an important catalyst for stimulating men's programs in clubs and congregations and will, we hope, serve as the germ of other programming ideas."

After the convention, Steve Davidoff, a member of my Philadelphia area congregation, who was inaugurated as president of the FJMC that year, made it his mission to raise the money to get the project off the ground. We approached Evelyn Berger, also a member of our synagogue, whose husband Bernie had recently died, and invited her to help by dedicating the first volume, Our Fathers Ourselves, in Bernie's memory. Evelyn loved the idea, and we were ready to launch the project.

One of the notable aspects of the "Hearing Men's Voices" volumes is that they are structured with important articles intended to be both thought and emotion provoking. They also include lesson plans that lay leaders could use to run sessions in their own clubs. This structure allowed the program to proliferate into our various communities without requiring a major expenditure of money that a club might not be able to afford, and encouraged local leaders to use their own talents. Most of all, it focused on the revelatory discussions that emerge when men get together and are able to talk about their emotions safely, without fear of embarrassment, in each other's presence.

"Hearing Men's Voices" has been one of the most compelling programs of the FJMC. It has infused programming with challenging purpose, and changed the lives of many men. It has been a vehicle for men to explore who they are, what role they play in society, the conflicting emotions they deal with, and the course they need to travel to become better men and better human beings.

Rabbi Seymour Rosenbloom is the retired rabbi of Congregation Adath Jeshurun, near Philadelphia.

GOING STRONG AFTER TWENTY YEARS

When Rabbi Seymour Rosenbloom addressed the FJMC International Convention in 1993 and shared some of his experiences working with the men of his congregation about the important issues in their lives the impact was dramatic. It was clear that the men who were in attendance that week at Split Rock had experienced what for many was a life changing experience. Imagine – men having the opportunity to openly discuss very personal and meaningful concerns with other men – extraordinary!

The warm response to Rabbi Rosenbloom generated a series of conversations, meetings and "think-tanks" that would ultimately result in the presentation of a new FJMC initiative "Hearing Men's Voices" at the biennial convention in 1997. We were able to identify six large categories for further discussion. These were:

1. "Body and Spirit" – Men's health
2. "Man Doesn't Live by Bread Alone" – The role of work in our lives
3. "Men in Search of God" – Spiritual experiences
4. "Heroes, Lovers and Friends" – Relationships
5. "Our Fathers Ourselves" – Our roles as fathers and sons
6. "The Egalitarian Synagogue" – Men's place in a changing environment

We recruited six talented writers (including Rabbi Rosenbloom) to create templates for discussion around these issues. A prototype booklet was prepared and distributed to the men at the convention. After another stirring and stimulating address by Rabbi Rosenbloom, breakout sessions were convened, led by the men who created the six discussion guides. It was not clear from the outset how the men would react to being involved in a small discussion group about often intimate matters. Yes, it worked with Rabbi Rosenbloom in his own community but would that success carry over to a wider FJMC audience? The response was overwhelming! By the end of many of these sessions, men were linked arm-and-arm, singing "Hinei Ma Tov" often with tears in their eyes. FJMC had struck a nerve and opened a gateway for discussion, fellowship and meaning for an entire new generation of men's club members.

The success of the "Hearing Men's Voices" pilot at the Concord convention started the ball rolling for what would become a series of workbooks providing with users a step-by-step guide to implementing a successful HMV program in their own communities. First in the series was <u>Our Fathers Ourselves – What Do We Want From Our Fathers? What Do They Need From Us?</u> With discussion topics ranging from "The First Kiss" (Rabbi Rosenbloom's program from our convention), to consideration of "The Wicked Child" to "Writing an Ethical Will" and more, this first guide in the series brought "Hearing Men's Voices" to communities across North America. Other guides in the series were produced over the following years exploring the major themes that were introduced at the 1997 convention.

Men's clubs quickly and enthusiastically adopted this program. It provided a safe place for men to explore the important issues in their lives. It also provided the basis for development of a community of men. This strengthened the men's club and ultimately the synagogue community as well.

"Hearing Men's Voices" has become a staple not only of the FJMC's biennial convention, but of regional retreats as well. The increasing visibility of the program also brought new challenges. While the programs themselves were of interest, many clubs asked for assistance in implementing HMV in their communities. As a result, in addition to experiencing "Hearing Men's Voices" at a convention or retreat, training programs were devised to develop leaders who could guide the implementation on the local level. Over the past few years several dozen "Mentschen" (as the HMV consultations were dubbed) were trained and remain an invaluable resource to communities looking to develop a program at their own clubs.

"Hearing Men's Voices" materials culminated in a book-length publication released in conjunction with the FJMC convention in Boston in 2013. Entitled <u>Jewish Men at the Crossroads</u>, this new book included some of the essays and discussion guides from the earlier publications but also featured new material written by influential writers from the religious and secular communities. <u>Jewish Men</u> was divided into sections mirroring the very first prototype. Each section concluded with new questions that could serve as a basis for discussion in an HMV forum. As is the FJMC style, an implementation guide was also developed in conjunction with this book and widely available through the FJMC website.

"Hearing Men's Voices" continues to evolve through the creativity of the men's clubs which have taken the program to heart. Men are now seen having meaningful discussions, not only in synagogue meeting rooms, but in private homes, pubs and other venues that are conducive for conversation. The original topic areas have expanded as well. When men began talking about the challenges of intermarriage in their families it was clear that a sensitive nerve had been touched. These discussions led to the separate development of FJMC's Keruv initiative (as discussed elsewhere in this volume). Clubs have broadening "Hearing Men's Voices" conversations to cover such varied topics as High Holiday experiences, politics, Jewish humor and so much more.

"Hearing Men's Voices" has provided a rallying cry for the men of the community for twenty years! It has been a wonderful way for men to create community and to get involved in Jewish life generally. The HMV team of Mentschen continues to explore and develop new ways and new venues for men's voices to be heard. An innovative program developed by one club has, through the work of FJMC, spread to more than 100 clubs in North America and is now being adopted overseas. As individual clubs develop their own variations, it's clear that after twenty years, the story of HMV is far from over.

Robert Braitman, M.D. is a former international president of FJMC and the editor of most of the HMV books.

MAKING IT YOUR OWN

A recent poll asked FJMC leaders which programs they most identified with the organization. Surprisingly, but not shockingly, the number one response was "Hearing Men's Voices." Twenty years after its inception, at a time when it was uncertain if men would truly be willing to speak to each other honestly about meaningful issues, HMV is now considered one of the central programs of the Men's Club movement. There are certainly many reasons for such success, including the ease of running a session, universality of the topics, low to no cost for putting it on, adaptability to any size group, and the powerful impact HMV has on its participants. It was for all these reasons that our club (Temple Israel in Sharon, Massachusetts) dove into HMV head first, in the deep end, and came to realize that one of the greatest strengths of the initiative was the ability to go beyond the manuals and make the discussions particularly unique and relevant to our members. We reveled in making HMV our own signature program and sharing those ideas with all who were interested. It is my firm belief that such a decision is one of the reasons why our club has achieved at the highest levels of the FJMC organization.

Making HMV your own may seem challenging at first, but once you get started, the only issue is trying to narrow down the infinite choices ahead of you. We were early adopters of HMV and followed each of the FJMC manuals exactly, providing us with a number of years of programming. By our fifth or sixth year, we found that we had covered the majority of topics laid out by FJMC, yet our members wanted more. We had some shifts in leadership in our HMV program and this offered a perfect opportunity to adopt a new approach. What followed led to a systematic and creative approach to running HMV which led to some incredible discussions, solidifying HMV as our key program, expanding to include other clubs in our area, and becoming a national model for how to evolve the original concept.

We began to meet each spring to plan a series for the upcoming year and would develop a theme of interest, crafting six sessions per year that fit the model. Part of the success of our approach was choosing to hold the meetings in a different person's home for each gathering. A registrar would be selected whose job involved nothing more than taking RSVPs and communicating with the host, facilitator, and organizers. Lastly, a facilitator was chosen based on an ability to engage others in discussion, not based on content expertise. For example, one of our most interactive sessions was run by a member who was a DJ, someone whose job depends on getting people involved. Airing different ideas would lead to discussion as to which series we would choose in a given year. Ideas were suggested which would hit a nerve or might push a boundary. Our first original series took on the topic of identity. Sessions touched on elements of occupational, physical, generational, spiritual, relational, and internal identity and all of its ramifications. What better way to start our own material than exploring our identities?

That first season was a hit and we then moved on to something more challenging – relationships. Sessions touched on everything from experiences with co-workers, to bullies, to reminiscing about dating, and to being open and honest about the relationships we have with our religious leaders. A key was touching on areas that most everyone had experience with, and providing a range of intimacy in terms of the topics. It was easy to talk about relationships at work, but more challenging to address being bullied or actually being a bully. With greater emotional depth involved in some of the talks, men were moved to laugh as well as to cry. The shared affect only served to strengthen the bonds of the participants, as well as the drive for more such programs.

In the following years, we touched on themes including how men connect with one another, whether through achievement, sports, food, family, humor, or Judaism. The humor session eventually devolved into a two hour riot of sharing jokes and funny life stories in which peoples' stomachs hurt from laughing so much. It's hard to describe the camaraderie which develops when guys get together month in and month out to share something important. We later focused on Jewish holidays and all the memories, traditions, and feelings they engender. Another year covered the theme of entertainment, from TV, to professional sports, movies, and how Jews are depicted onscreen.

Based on the wonderful book by Ron Wolfson, The Seven Questions You're Asked in Heaven, we did a series with each session covering one of the questions. The ideas for programs are infinite and can be inspired by most anything. In 2015 a young man from our town, Ezra Schwartz, was shot dead by a terrorist in the West Bank while on a school trip. With frayed nerves and angst about political uncertainty and international terror, we put together an HMV program called "Politically Incorrect." This was a highly charged program which addressed feelings about the election process, how terror has impacted our lives, and Muslim and Jewish relations. Such a discussion is not for the beginning club, but it offered a safe haven to voice raw feelings, some of which truly would be termed politically incorrect, but which captured a crucial moment in our lives. HMV provided the safe vehicle for us to vent, commiserate, and find strength from one another. Our latest program was dedicated to making prayer more personal by exploring our experiences and feelings about prayers and times when we pray. The overwhelming sense was that this brought a greater appreciation for how and why we use prayer, and increased understanding of the meanings we attribute to prayer.

The range of experiences, topics, and levels of engagement in HMV has surpassed our hopes over the years. We have made it our own signature program and as a result, we have become one of the strongest clubs in the FJMC. Without HMV, we never would have come to know each other so well, or to be able to find a way to voice our thoughts and feelings about so many things in a supportive environment. We have taken to inviting other area clubs to join us to share in the experience, and a number of them have now learned of the power of honest discussion among men.

As simple as it may seem, sharing openly about whatever is important to our group in a given year has solidified our affiliations with each other, our club, shul, and our faith. When we see someone at Kiddush and ask "How are you doing?" we mean it, as we know what is going on beneath the surface for so many of our members. Those ties have led to an unswerving commitment to continuing to push the boundaries of what our members will share, and in turn spreading the word to other clubs and regions through trainings and developing supporting materials. Three of our club members have been part of the FJMC HMV committee for years. We truly believe that there is no more flexible, creative FJMC program in existence today. At little to no cost, but much creative energy, we have been able to utilize HMV to help improve the quality of relationships among men, a boost to mental health by offering a means to emote with friends, and added vibrancy to our club.

Dr. Paul Davidson is a member of Temple Israel, Sharon, Massachusetts.

FROM THE RECORD

MAKING IT YOUR OWN

HOW ARE WE TO RESPOND?

We hear about new communities all the time – whether grouped by religion, gender, sexual preference, geography, socioeconomic group or family profile. Each of these communities has its own sets of special interests, its own agenda and special needs. **Somehow, many of us never understood the need for the definition of a community of men. What are our special interests, our unique needs, our challenges?...**

This implementation guide is the first of a series that will provide your club programming opportunities in this important area. The focal points that have been developed for this program were selected because they address various aspects of male behavior that emerge on a continuous basis.

These materials will also guide you toward programmatic events in your own Men's Clubs. I believe this type of programming will provide a refocused mission that will enhance men's roles in the synagogue, and liberate men to be themselves.

From the preface to <u>Our Fathers Ourselves</u> by Robert E. Braitman, M.D.

COMMUNICATING WITH YOUR TEENAGER

It is understandable for adolescents, usually those on the verge of puberty, to shy away when a father seeks to place his hands on their heads. At this age, being touched by your parents – particularly in public – wouldn't be "cool."

Teenagers will tolerate almost anything if one doesn't ask too many questions or probe too deeply. They will understand the lesson and the affection which is transmitted through the bestowing of a blessing, even though they might choose not to articulate their feelings.

From program material, <u>Our Fathers Ourselves</u>.

BEING A JEWISH MAN

Perhaps the time has come for us to examine Torah lessons with an eye toward how they can guide us as men to make critical decisions in the boardrooms, the family room and in the bedroom. Abraham faced the call to uproot himself in midlife and knew the trials of a blended family. Isaac was almost sacrificed for his father's beliefs. Ishmael was a rejected son, Joseph a favorite, and each suffered for it. Elderly Boaz was involved in a December-May relationship with Ruth, while the Judge Samuel was forcibly retired. The richness of these tales combined with the insights of Halacha (Jewish law) can instruct us as we face the twist and turns inherent in a man's life.

How shall we pray and for what shall we pray? Many voices in the Women's Movement decry the fact that God is always described in male metaphors: Lord, Father, King, Master, Man of War. Perhaps we as men might also have mixed feelings about praying to God in these terms given our own experiences having fathers and being fathers, supervisors, soldiers, etc.

From the Introduction, Listening to God's Voice, Rabbi Howard A. Addison.

WHY DON'T MEN SEEK HEALTH CARE?

I asked this question to my friend Gerald Evans. Gerry is the founder and director of the Men's Resource Center in Philadelphia....

Gerry has given the issue of men's cavalier attitudes about their health a lot of thought. "It all starts with a man's being out of touch with his own emotions. He spends so much time ignoring his feelings, he has difficulty identifying them. He doesn't recognize or acknowledge the cues his body is giving him."

We grow up keeping our cards close to the vest. We don't want to give anything away. We need to appear strong, invulnerable to others. We have to convince ourselves, too. So when we encounter a pain, when we find our abilities compromised, our first impulse is denial.

From a program handout by Rabbi Seymour Rosenbloom for Body & Spirit: Men Staying Healthy and Fit.

ARE WE WHAT WE DO?

How would you answer these questions: Do you get more excited about your work than about your family or anything else? Do you take work with you to bed? On weekends? On vacation? Is work the activity you like to do best and talk about most? Do you work more than 40 hours a week? Have your family or friends given up expecting you on time? Do you believe that it is okay to work long hours if you love what you're doing? Are you afraid that if you don't work hard you will lose your job or be a failure? ...

What is the place of work in our lives? Let me use three Hebrew words: *eved, oved,* and *avodah*. Are you an *eved*, a slave, or an *oved*, a worker, or are you engaged in *avodah*, in sacred tasks? The choices we make provide the answer and make clear where we place our priorities and where we put work in our lives.

From an essay by Rabbi Howard Lifshitz in Work & Worth.

APPENDIX: I LOVE CHUCK

This volume has been designed as a Festschrift, a collection of serious articles on the subject of the initiatives of the Federation of Jewish Men's Club upon the occasion of the retirement of executive director Rabbi Charles Simon. Personal messages and good wishes would be out of place in a traditional volume of that nature, but then one of the hallmarks of Rabbi Simon's tenure has been refusing to be locked into conventional thinking. His friends and colleagues would not be denied the opportunity to express their feelings. Thus we provide this appendix, where those expressions could be given free rein.

THRIVING JEWS

A Festschrift is an interesting thing. Compiled to recognize an individual deserving of praise, these volumes normally contain academic articles written about topics in the field of study most closely associated with the honoree. To honor Rabbi Charles Simon with such an academic article would be terribly out of place. For "Chuck," as he is belovedly called by his "guys" – his legion of admirers in the Federation of Jewish Men's Clubs – has compiled a resume that is anything but "normal." It is, in fact, extraordinary.

I first met Chuck in 1969. We were both enrolled in the Mechinah summer program at the Jewish Theological Seminary of America. This was a preparatory step before rabbinical school. The summer was filled with wonderful learning and great conversations about the tumultuous times we lived in; the country was still reeling from the momentous year of 1968. The winds of change were howling throughout the land, including in the Jewish community. Chuck and I became good friends that summer, but honestly, who knew if our paths would cross again? Who could have imagined, certainly not I, that some sixteen years later, we would work together on a project that had the audacious goal of changing the Jewish lives of thousands of individuals and families?

Chuck has always demonstrated a remarkably consistent and clear mission, a mission that has propelled him to the very top of my short list of truly great Jewish community leaders: to bring Jews and those in relationship with Jews closer to Jewish practice and ideas. The Hebrew word for bringing people closer to Judaism is "keruv." Well before any Pew Study, well before any debates about how to welcome the intermarrieds in our midst, well before talk of synagogue transformation, Chuck knew that the most urgent need of the moment was to empower people to engage with Judaism, to help them see how Judaism and Jewish practice could lead them to a life of meaning and purpose, belonging and blessing.

From the minute Chuck graduated from rabbinical school, he looked for a platform to do this work. Luckily for the Conservative Movement and beyond, he found it in what was then a somewhat sleepy corner of synagogue life: men's groups which, in the years B.C. (Before Chuck), were mostly known for helping out with the daily minyan and putting on Sunday morning breakfasts. How did Chuck transform the Federation of Jewish

Men's Clubs into a vibrant and essential component of congregations? He devoted every day of his outstanding thirty-six year career to imbuing his guys with high purpose. It was obvious to Chuck that if synagogue life was to thrive, we needed thriving Jews – Jews who were knowledgeable and comfortable in their practice, both at the synagogue and in the home. And how would he achieve this? His genius insight was to turn the standard adult education model in synagogues upside down. Instead of top-down teaching, he insisted on bottom-up learning. Instead of him teaching Torah to his guys, he would inspire and guide his guys to teach Torah *to each other*. The result: an impressive list of national campaigns to motivate and equip his guys with educational models and resources that enabled them to participate fully and confidently in davening and ritual practice, unafraid to walk into any shul, inspired to celebrate Jewish moments in the home.

None of this would have happened without Chuck. I will leave it to my colleagues to extol the other influential achievements of Rabbi Charles Simon. Suffice it to say that Chuck has demonstrated how a rabbi with vision, intelligence, skill, and the willingness to confront the most urgent challenges of our time can become a cherished and respected leader of a movement and the Jewish people. Above all, he is the perfect exemplar of the critical importance of building relationships with his people and encouraging them to build relationships with each other. Spend five minutes at an FJMC convention and you will witness the hugs, the *ruach*, and the enthusiastic embrace of Jewish living. It is the reason so many of us adore and cherish this amazing man. It is the reason so many of us call him a beloved friend. It is the reason so many of us are unabashed to say: "I love this guy."

So, let me say it – loud and clear: "I love Chuck!" *Yi'asher kochacha* and *mazal tov*, my partner, my leader, my friend!

Dr. Ron Wolfson, Fingerhut Professor of Education, American Jewish University

CHUCK'S VISION

I love praying together with the Keruv group. Simple gestures like washing hands with prayers, lighting candles, flying napkins, are symbols of my Keruv experience with Chuck, now dear to my heart. Presenting at convention, becoming an expert on my love – grand parenting, sharing with other temples, leading trainings, have all strengthened my conviction, my confidence, my beliefs, my love, my unity with these wonderful people.

If at any time, any of us reach an impasse, or have a question, a dilemma, the rest of the Keruv network is but an email away. Chuck envisioned this. My cohorts at temple, and in life, are amazed at how fast a response can be obtained. "I need a mohel in the local area," I wrote to five people. In 10 minutes, I had a response. "What does your synagogue do regarded membership and dues?" Across the country, friends answer speedily. Chuck mentored this.

The Keruv initiative has started slowly in our synagogue. But we now have advanced the dance on the bima, created family membership, welcomed supportive spouses and families. We have a long way to go. But I do write an article in each bulletin and the presence of Keruv has become acknowledged. The congregants know what the word means. After 10 years, parents do acknowledge their children's weddings, births, and new relationships. More and more of the congregation are finding that they too have to be more inclusive in their family lives. What a vision Chuck had.

When my father died, Chuck came to Shiva at my house. That meant so much to me, solidifying my love for this man. A love and tradition I was honored to be able to pay forward.

I can truly say my involvement with Keruv has become a turning point in my life, making me a better, more caring, and more inclusive and respectful individual. The model and vision that Chuck created will forever be part of me. We need to continue this endeavor to reach more people. This has to be just the beginning – to carry on Chuck's work. And more important, Chuck, this new chapter for you is wonderful and healthy for you. With joy we wish you a beautiful retirement. But please remember, we need to be part of it – some way.

Alayne Pick, Woodcliff Lake, New Jersey

AN APPRECIATION

There was a man who never learned to color within the lines. To this man, lines show the way things are. He colored life the way things should be.

The color palate he has created in his career is dazzling. Attend any FJMC event, and you will see Jewish men approach their Judaism with joy and enthusiasm. Tefillin have been transformed from discarded artifacts to vehicles of intimacy. Grace after meals, the oft forgotten prayer, has become a wake-up call that energizes the soul. The long forgotten Prophets have become history coming alive. A simple prayer like Aleinu creates choral opportunities for men who wouldn't be caught dead singing anywhere else. Men opening their hearts in sincere and meaningful conversation with each other is a social anomaly of major proportions. The display of colors in Charles Simon's palate is wider than words can capture.

One achievement stands out above the others. In an attempt to save the faith, Conservative Judaism has abandoned its people. Until Rabbi Simon crossed the established lines, Jews who married non-Jews were shunned and excluded from a place inside the tent of Conservative Judaism. I witnessed friends and relatives told by Conservative leaders to go elsewhere for their simchas, excluded from membership, ignored in publications, told to stand somewhere else (or to stand not at all), denied a place of respect, treated as human failures; all done to dissuade others from doing the same. Time has shown these lines to be a demarcation of failure.

Rabbi Simon crossed many lines when he created the Keruv movement within Conservative Judaism. His refusal to join his colleagues who behaved like lemmings bent on suicide, was an act of courage that alienated him from those he was closest to. At least initially. Through hard work and courage, he has bent the curve of history. Slowly like tectonic plates, the leadership of the Conservative movement creeps ever closer to embracing all Jews, regardless of whom they love. He leaves the job unfinished but headed in the right direction. As he enters the phase of his life with more time to focus on his personal directions, it is a good time for Conservative Judaism to reflect who will fill his shoes. Who will pick-up his mantle to question the way things are? Who will have the courage to challenge authority? Who else knows how to color outside the lines?

Art Spar, West End Synagogue, New York City

YOU ARE A NATURAL

Your impact has changed lives. You are approachable, non-judgmental… your goodness comes from your heart and soul. You are a natural! You are one of those rare humans beings with an innate sense of knowing the right thing to do in comforting, welcoming and giving others the courage to be self-actualizing.

You have given those who have put their "hats in the Keruv Corner," the courage and the know-how to do the right thing in the right way. You have enabled and given the tools to those who take the plunge… you see in people beyond the capacities they see in themselves. Through the Keruv/Understanding Intermarriage Initiative you have given new life to the Jewish Community as a whole, and to the individuals who have been fortunate to be part of our culture.

We all want to be in your company, you make us feel comfortable and at ease. You are exciting and dynamic. We want to be loved by you, and you have it in your heart to comply. You are easy to please, you don't set conditions. You unconditionally love each one of us. You accept where we are at, and give us the room to move forward, to shine, to do the best we can… and then some! You do it all with ease as an equal. You are a moral man. By example you set the mark. The Jewish world is better for your being a caring leader and a gadfly.

As a Rabbi and teacher you are a gift to all who have been fortunate to be part of your life. Thank you, Chuck.

Lynne Wolfe, Alliance of Jewish Intermarriage Outreach Professionals
FJMC Keruv Coordinator, Walnut Creek, California

AN UNCANNY KNACK

Meeting Rabbi Simon in 2003 turned out to be a life changing event for me. Chuck, as his friends call him, has become a special part of many of our lives. He is a mentor, a friend, and has challenged his Keruv family to make a difference in the Conservative movement. And what a difference we have made.

We began to shed the aversive image that was created. Now we are beginning to enjoy the fruits of 14 years of cultural change. With our outreach we have given the tools to synagogues and rabbis to change their culture, their websites, and lead a new generation of Conservative Jewish thought and practice.

I saw Chuck give so many people a chance to express themselves. I was one of those people. He has an uncanny knack of how to recognize talent and, most of all, develop people.

One day at the international convention in 2003 Chuck approached me. Although he never had met me, he asked if I would be willing to train as a Keruv consultant. I was taken back because that was the furthest thing from my mind. I decided to step out of the box and say yes. Eventually I became co-chair of the FJMC Keruv initiative. The skills I took from what I learned helped me move up to the upper echelon' of FJMC including VP of FJMC and the Chairman of the Foundation for Jewish Life. Chuck's guidance and constant communication allowed myself and others to work together to create and innovate this emerging Keruv model.

We took a trip to Latin America and the Amazon with Chuck. What a trip it was.

We met a Jewish Community in the Amazon. It was an eye opening experience that I still cherish today. All of us on the trip were touched by what we learned and became involved in. This was all part of a plan Chuck had to build Latin American relations with an eye on reviving the Latin American Jewish Community. We have expanded FJMC to a much larger presence with clubs in Canada, India, Israel, Uganda, France, Chile and more.

"Make a difference in people's life!" This defines the legacy that Rabbi Simon leaves. Over these last fourteen years, I have watched the transformation of both an organization and a movement. Judaism needs people like Chuck who dedicate their lives with warmth and passion. Chuck defines the true meaning in my mind of a leader.

The best way to create value for yourself is to create value for others. Chuck has done this naturally.

Gary Smith, Adath Israel, Cincinnati, Ohio

WARM, NON-JUDGMENTAL AND REALLY FUNNY

My husband and I met Rabbi Simon at our first Keruv convention in Chicago in 2015. Although we have known him for only two short years, we immediately felt a connection with him that makes it seem like we've been friends forever. We admire him for many reasons. He truly accepts our interfaith family and understands the struggles that we've encountered attempting to provide a Jewish household for our children. He is warm, non-judgmental and really funny. He is smart, charismatic, an incredible leader and always willing to help others. We share his passion for red wine which has kept us up way too late at night during our visits with him as we discuss the world's problems and how we can solve them.

Rabbi Simon is truly a mensch. Although he is retiring from FJMC, his passion for the Keruv movement will live on through the Keruv Consultants that he trained and through the many, many people that have been touched by him throughout his lifetime. We suspect that he will continue traveling throughout the world sharing his expertise and wisdom with others, while sampling the best wine that each country has to offer. We hope he invites us with him!

Maurine & Jacob Halpern, Temple Beth El, Birmingham, Alabama

A ROLE MODEL

Rabbi, during the course of the roughly 15 years we have known one another, you have been an inspiration and a role model to me. Through my various activities in FJMC, but most especially the Keruv initiative, my life has been transformed, as a Jew, community leader, spouse, and parent. I can't truly put into words the value that you personally, and FJMC in general, have added to my life.

With respect to Keruv, it was a privilege to accompany you and partner with you on this important initiative, from its earliest days as a member of its "Think Tank." The transformation I referenced above has been repeated through the rabbinic and lay leader training activities and then in our synagogues and in their member families, as well as in the Conservative movement. None of us will ever be the same (and by that, of course, I mean a very good thing). When I interact with a Keruv family in our shul that I have worked with, and get invited to their son's bar mitzvah and spend time with the non-Jewish spouse in our Men's Club activities, I see you and think about you and the impact you have indirectly had on their lives. On their behalf as well as my own, thank you so much.

Peter Gotlieb, Beth Shalom, Livingston, New Jersey

CHANGING A CULTURE

I could extol my delight at having had the privilege of being a positive influence, no matter how slight, on my synagogue and on Conservative Judaism. Rarely does one have an opportunity to have such an impact on something so important. But the mission of Keruv and the brilliant direction and nurturing of it by you, Chuck, has enabled so many of us to have savored the opportunity and satisfaction of gradually changing a culture that not only strengthens Judaism in this country but increases the potential for happiness amongst its members. These have all provided enormous joy for me to serve in the capacity of a representative of this movement.

But what I'd really like to discuss here are the contributions that Rabbi Charles Simon has made in allowing me to better understand and appreciate my faith. Practically every time I've had the opportunity to participate in a service led by him, I've been treated with expansive and probing discussions on biblical passages, on explanations of how different Haftarah evolved, of why certain prayers in our liturgy appear as they do. It seems odd to be marveling at the kind of scholarship one might expect to come primarily from a pulpit rabbi which Chuck has not been for several decades. But I think that it is a testament to a roving, curious mind that Charles Simon has been able to effect such emotion, contemplation and wonder for our sacred texts. One can easily fall into a rote kind of ennui at repeating such things Shabbat after Shabbat and indeed, that's the road that I was heading down in my own observance. But it has been Chuck's own sense of fascination, wonderment and scholarship that has periodically nudged me from such a tired path and provided new insights and affection for my faith. I say this in admiration both because of my own struggles as an educator at promoting such inspiration in my students but also because I know that this is related somehow but separate from his incredible work at promoting openness and welcoming in our shuls.

Of the many mitzvahs we Jews are supposed to engage in, *Tikkun Olam* – repairing the world – has always seemed to me to be the most challenging to accomplish. However, I can think of no better guide for how to take on such an essential but Sisyphean task than to observe and, to the best of my own limited abilities, emulate the examples provided by Rabbi Charles Simon.

David Mogul, Beth Hillel Congregation Bnai Emunah, Winnetka, Illinois

BELIEVING IN OURSELVES

The bottom line is this: Chuck is the first Rabbi ever to make me feel like it was more than just, "okay," to be me as a Jew. Instead, he made me believe I am an asset to the Conservative movement. Not only that I have a place in it, but that I should be a leader – a thought leader – of it. Because of Chuck, I am sure that my goals and actions are both noble and for the greater good of Conservative Judaism as well. Supportive isn't the right word. Chuck's sincerity, loyalty and insight make us believe in ourselves. Watching, listening to and learning from him has made me more courageous, more empathetic, more driven, more honest and simply a better person..

From a place deep in my heart that rarely shows itself: Thank you for the years of guidance, friendship and light. I am better, Conservative Judaism is better, and the world is better because we have you.

Liz Cox, Beth Torah, Richardson, Texas

CONNECTING TO JUDAISM

From the moment I met you (and the "Keruv Crew") I had no idea the impact that FJMC and the Keruv Imitative would have on our family. Chuck, you were able to mobilize a passionate group of men and women who challenged the status quo of the Conservative movement – and I am fortunate to have been a Keruv Consultant. From your dedication to inclusion, your inspirational articles and books, Michael and I were able to envision and experience a rich Jewish family life that included a deep and meaningful connection to our synagogue – despite the fact that we were an interfaith couple. The choreography of the synagogue became accessible to us and we were motivated to remodel and revitalize our congregational vision of welcoming.

We connected to Judaism in a way that we never dreamed possible – Keruv Shabbat, Passover University and Hearing Our Voices. Chuck, not only did Keruv reinvigorate my connection to Judaism, it also gave Michael the confidence and competence to convert after 18 years of marriage. I can't thank you enough for all you have done for us. We wish you all the best in this next chapter of your life!

Rochelle & Michael Sullivan, Beth Israel, Owings Mills, Maryland

A PIONEER

From 2008-2012, I had the pleasure of being Chairman of the Conservative movement-wide attempt at a Keruv Initiative. The visionary thinker behind this initiative, which the Federation of Jewish Men's Clubs began about a decade before, was Chuck Simon. More than any other person in our Movement, Chuck had the insight and the wisdom to understand the various and interconnected issues of interfaith couples, families, grandparents and, frankly, non-Jewish in-laws and kin. He has made a difference in the lives of intermarried families. Indeed, he is one of the gems of our movement.

It has been a true task, convincing Conservative movement leadership of the wisdom of Chuck's insights. Chuck has been a pioneer. And like other pioneers for a cause, this opportunity became a challenge, which in turn became a cause, an advocacy and even a calling. Few know better than I what he went through advocating for Keruv. Because of this, because of my long relationship with Chuck and the road we and others have walked together, I have come to regard Chuck as a true hero and a giant.

None of us know what lies ahead on the road we choose to travel. Chuck, I wish only for you good health, good fortune and good friends along the way.

Rabbi Bob Slosberg, Adath Jeshurun, Louisville, Kentucky

THE FLAMINGO BAR

I met Rabbi Chuck Simon in the famous Flamingo Bar at the Concord during my first Rabbinical Assembly Convention in 1993. Interestingly, there was no one at the bar but Chuck and me. We began our relationship and friendship at that moment in that place. Since that fortuitous encounter our friendship and my respect and affection for Chuck have only grown.

We discovered that we shared a very good friend. For me, it was someone I knew from preschool and for Chuck, his college roommate at Wisconsin. It is one of the great ironies of the world that our mutual friend who had two rabbis as good, old friends took photos of nude women for his wife, who is an artist — this is what he does for a living. Chuck and I went on to become rabbis.

I realized in the Flamingo Bar almost twenty five years ago that I was with a person with vision, courage and dedication. I did not know then how Chuck would inspire and challenge me (us) and charge me (us) to always try thinking ahead as to what is best for our Conservative movement and our Jewish people.

Chuck and our then Brotherhood president, Dr. Gary Smith, got me and our congregation in on the ground floor of the Keruv program. Keruv is one of the most important and sea-changing developments in Conservative Judaism in recent times and we owe all of this to Chuck. I was honored to present at Keruv conferences and to host and facilitate several in Cincinnati. Keruv, thanks to Chuck, led me and so many colleagues to rethink our understanding of and positions on interfaith issues in our times and in our synagogues. I thank Chuck for doing so even though, as many know, it wasn't always easy.

Chuck pushed us as he has with many other concerns. He zeroes in on critical issues and does so in creative and innovative ways and has done this for years in his service to our movement and our people. He makes us step back and think, reconsider, and look at things differently. This is why we respect, value and appreciated him so much; this is why Rabbi Charles Simon is our teacher and our leader.

My only regret is that in recent years I have not been able to be with Chuck as much as I was some years ago. Kathy and I were fondly reminiscing when he stayed in our home and honored our synagogue several times by being with us for Shabbat. I hope to turn this around and spend time with Chuck as I look forward to my own retirement.

I, along with so many, share our prayers and blessings with Chuck and most of all our thankfulness for who he is, all that he has given and all that he has inspired and created.

Chuck, you're the man!

May you go from strength to strength, from mitzvah to mitzvah and be nourished by all that you have merited and earned.

Rabbi Irv Wise, Adath Israel, Cincinnati, Ohio

THINK TANKS

Years ago, as the last Rabbinical Assembly convention at the Concord Hotel concluded, three young rabbis sat under the gazebo on the front lawn, absorbing the scene as their colleagues and families left the grand resort. It was a sad moment. The three friends recognized the tremendous change approaching. As the R.A. conventions would travel around the Conservative world, we would be confronted by modern challenges to the way we viewed Jewish life from our 3080 Broadway-to-Concord cocoon.

Questions were abundant. Would we become a truly egalitarian movement? How would we approach issues of sexual identity? The three rabbis sitting together that afternoon decided that the issue which would haunt us, would be how we responded to the rising rate of dual faith marriages. Do we welcome dual faith families? Do we maintain our total commitment to endogamy? Are we willing to lose our children by turning our backs on them because they marry spouses who are not Jewish and do not wish to convert?

While many in our movement discuss finding answers to issues revolving around intermarriage, it was the Federation of Jewish Men's Clubs, under the guidance of Rabbi Chuck Simon (one of those three young Rabbis) that has led this conversation for almost two decades.

For years, Chuck brought Conservative rabbis together in small groups. These "Think Tanks" brought rabbis from outlying congregations into contact with leaders of the movement. Together we discussed ways to open our Jewish tent flaps, to continue the tradition of our Father Abraham's welcoming tent. We met all over the country. No topics were forbidden. Conversations were lively, informed and important to all. Some minds were changed. Others held to their views. Men and women of strong faith came together as colleagues and friends. We talked. We argued. We sought what we each hoped would be the path for our movement to open gateways while holding true to our ideals.

Leviticus 19:18 teaches us: "Love your fellow as yourself." The Torah commands us to love those like us as we love ourselves. The Torah continues in verse 34: "The stranger who resides with you shall be to you as one of your citizens; you shall love him as you love yourself." Here the command v'ahavtah, you shall love, obviously refers to people who are not like us, those who are not Jewish. The third v'ahavtah is found in Deuteronomy: "You shall love the Lord your God." I believe that Keruv shows both love of our fellows and love of others. I believe that the innovations and creativity we see across the Conservative movement in discovering ways to welcome our children and their families are proof that our love of God is the reason to perform Keruv. "Tradition and Change" still works.

Keruv is just one of the great initiatives that FJMC has undertaken with Chuck. FJMC has benefitted greatly from Chuck's energy, creativity and daring to do what is right. May you always grow from strength to strength, discovering new challenges and interests every day.

Rabbi Murray Ezring, Temple Israel, Charlotte, North Carolina

MULTI-TASKING IS HIS MIDDLE NAME

I have had the privilege of knowing Chuck for 40 years. First, we taught together at the Hebrew High School of Temple Israel of Great Neck, where his creativity was already evident. Since then we have been rabbinic colleagues and good friends. In the 1990's he gave me the opportunity to help build Masorti UK while he built Masorti France.

During his long tenure as Executive Director of FJMC, I watched him build a strong Federation, utilizing his unique talents of innovation and creativity. He broke new ground on a multitude of levels with programs that continue to inspire and benefit our movement worldwide. Congregation Beth Shalom of Northbrook, where I was the Senior Rabbi for 35 years, has embraced many of Chuck's programs, most notably Keruv. The synagogue has been an active participant in it and has become a more inclusive and welcoming congregation because of Keruv. Chuck has spoken there and captivated and motivated the community each time. He seems to be able to be everywhere at the same time; multi-tasking is his middle name.

His multi-tasking includes continued involvement with our movement worldwide, especially in France, the Yellow Candle Program and so much more. He is always thinking outside the box and never runs out of the energy to care about and do for others. Chuck manages to be there in a supportive role for all of us, clergy and congregant alike, all the time and is an endless source of new ideas.

Chuck - I cherish our friendship which has spanned more than half of our lives. I will always be grateful for the significant role you have played in my own successful rabbinate and admire how much you have added to the growth and vitality of our movement around the world. May your retirement give you the richly deserved time and freedom to choose new directions and seek new opportunities for self-fulfillment. May God bless you and your family with long life and good health in the long years to come.

Rabbi Carl Wolkin (ret.), Congregation Beth Shalom, Northbrook, Illinois

A RENAISSANCE MAN

Rabbi Charles Simon is truly a Renaissance man. While many may extol his vision for American Jewry, for inspiring several generations of men, for being a gadfly for reinterpretation, and rejuvenated your soul, most impressive to me is his ability to absorb vast amounts of scholarship and academic studies and to translate them into meaningful and memorable stories of us—who we were, who we are.

His delightful study Royalty, Religion, Sex and Mystery (2016) masterfully tells our story from the Ark of the Covenant to the first century of the Common Era in approximately 110 pages. Rabbi Simon picks significant snippets from our story and relates them in interesting and memorable ways. For example the story of the Ark of the Covenant is told in the first person. Some snippets are related in the voice of a close relative.

His book, Biblical Leadership after Moses, again in approximately hundred pages, deals with short memorable snippets of our biblical ancestors. The good, the bad, the ugly, pimples and all. Again told with delightful and eminently readable prose.

Understanding of the Haftarot suggests a nexus theory for understanding the relationship between the haftorot and relating them to the Torah portions. I carry this in my talis zekel and frequently refer to it. It wonderfully goes into the political social history. His style is to present it in bite-size portions and snippets. Behind these snippets are a synthesis and presentation of much of the current critical thinking, archaeological evidence, historical research, social and political history and erudition.

But, masterful teacher that he is, Rabbi Simon challenges us to think on our own by asking us questions. How we approach each of these questions affects us on an individual basis. Sometimes he shows us some of his enormous ability for critical thinking. In a few short paragraphs he takes us from animal sacrifice to the precursors of our current prayer. Chuck's ability to present the snippets and questions to resonate in each of our individual capacities is truly a great gift from a teacher to us all.

Many years ago I started to study Judaics. For renewing my interest, I am grateful. Thank you, Chuck.

Michael Freilich, Beth Israel, Hunt Valley, Maryland

QUOD ERAT DEMONSTRANDUM

In my high school, it was the obligation of every student to study and master Euclidean Geometry. Euclid proceeded from a set of simple assumptions to demonstrate and prove how the world was constructed. At the end of every proof were the same three letters. Q.E.D. Quod erat demonstrandum. That which was to have been proven.

Has our Chuck made a difference in the world?

Are things now reflecting a construction that was just a bit different from before?

Are there actual individual people who are more inspired now to reach beyond themselves and make a positive and more constructive difference in the world of contemporary Conservative Judaism?

Q.E.D.

A friend of mine used to say, "If you are in the middle of the forest and totally lost, and someone offered you the choice of either a compass or a jungle guide, which would you choose?"

Everything we have done over these past 15-plus years have been with Chuck as our jungle guide. Knowing the direction has not been enough. Going forward, knowing the demographics and rabbinic proclivities and synagogue leadership fears will not be enough. God got lucky with Joshua. Hopefully, someone up there will sprinkle a bit of pixie dust on our venture and we will discover new energies to climb new mountains.

Godspeed, Chuck.

Harvey Braunstein

fjmc

Leadership Innovation Community

The FJMC mission is to involve Jewish Men in Jewish Life by building and strengthening Men's Clubs in the Conservative / Masorti Movement. We accomplish this mission by:

Leadership: mentoring leaders at the club, region and international level,

Innovation: developing programming that better connects people of all ages to the Jewish community,

Community: forming meaningful long-lasting relationships based on camaraderie, common interests and core values.

Federation of Jewish Men's Clubs
475 Riverside Drive, Suite 832
New York, NY 10115-0022
(212) 749-8100

Website: www.fjmc.org
Facebook: FJMC_HQ
Twitter: @FJMC_HQ
LinkedIn: http://www.linkedin.com/company/fjmc
E-mail: international@fjmc.org

www.ingramcontent.com/pod-product-compliance
Lightning Source LLC
Chambersburg PA
CBHW050531280326
41933CB00011B/1546